Rhysop's Fables

Two hundred and seven
unhelpful and irresponsible fables
for the modern age

plus the parable of a homeless fable

Rhys Hughes

(a man who was a toucan in a previous life)

Gloomy Seahorse Press

Gloomy Seahorse Press
http://gloomyseahorsepress.blogspot.com

Dedicated to

Aesop, Phaedrus, Jean de la Fontaine
and
Sissy Pantelis

Table of Contents

Foreword

Hello! How are you?

We all know that Aesop wrote fables; but he wasn't the only one. Hesiod and Archilochus preceded him, and a great many authors came after him. For example, the *Panchatantra* is an Indian collection of animal fables that was written down in the 3rd Century BC, possibly by the writer Vishnu Sharma. For centuries afterwards, other authors also attempted the composition of fables.

Phaedrus, the Roman fabulist, flourished in the 1st Century AD and was the first to write fables in Latin; Vardan Aygektsi was an Armenian priest who wrote fables in the 13th Century; Leonardo Da Vinci made his own contribution to the genre two hundred years later; and let us not forget Jean de la Fontaine, the most sophisticated fabulist of them all, who turned Aesop into delightful verse in the 17th Century.

Those are just a few authors who have accepted the challenge of writing fables. There were many others. Fables are for everyone. There's no reason why we can't all be fabulists! How fabulous is that?

So please find here a selection of my own fables. In keeping with tradition, each one is followed by a brief moral; but most of my morals are amoral or even immoral. Unlike the authors mentioned above, I have decided to write a set of *irresponsible* fables...

Irresponsibility gets a bad press. But an irresponsible action can be just as potent a gesture of defiance against authority as more controlled and rational opposition. In the particular case of these fables, 'authority' includes moral fabulists: all those sages and gurus who pretend to have the answers to the meaning of life.

There are no answers to life, because life isn't a question...

Anyway, I hope you will enjoy what follows and that you will find at least some wit and wisdom (or anti-wisdom) in my fables. There are 207 of them and if you fail to find the sequence entertaining, kindly remember this other fable that I made up just now:

There once was a reader who didn't like the fables that he read. He was so dismayed that he began shouting and waving his arms. The vibrations of his tantrum caused all the heavy pots and pans on the shelf above him to fall onto his head. As he lay in agony on the floor, bleeding from a serious head wound, he lamented to himself, "How I wish I had been less pompous and critical! But now it's too late for such regrets and I am doomed!"

Thanks for listening!

Rhysop's Fables

1 POLISHING OFF THE BOSS

A business tycoon who owned a large warehouse full of machines, tools and assorted implements hired a casual labourer to clean the merchandise so it could be sold at a higher price. "Polish every item but make sure you buff the undersides as well," he said.

The casual labourer stepped inside the warehouse and was astonished at the clutter he beheld. To save time he decided to dig a tunnel under the warehouse and excavate a large cavern there, so that he might clean the specified undersides with less trouble.

Shortly after this task was completed, the business tycoon entered the warehouse to inspect the casual labourer's work. The weight of his body was just enough to cause the weakened floor to give way and he was sent plummeting into the empty space below.

¶ If you give vague instructions to an amateur, sooner or later you will find yourself falling fatally into a hole.

2 SALAD DAYS

A fox and a carrot were the best of friends. One day the carrot said, "Our friendship must finally come to an end. My master told me that he plans to grate me over his next salad and splash me with oil and vinegar. Such an honour has elevated my status to the point where I should no longer be seen in your company. So farewell!"

The fox was filled with envy at these words and, unbeknownst to the carrot, he crept into the master's house and curled up tightly in the salad bowl. But when the master returned home and saw him there, he chased him away with curses and howls!

¶ Just because something is an orangey-red colour doesn't mean it goes well with lettuce and cucumber.

3 NOTHING TO CROW ABOUT

A crow sitting on the branch of an oak was amazed when a scarecrow sat at the base of the tree and began unwrapping a cloth that contained all the ingredients of a picnic. "Hey, are you willing to share any of that?" cried the crow, more as a joke than a serious question, for he didn't believe the scarecrow would be happy to give part of his feast to the very creature he was supposed to scare away. "Certainly," replied the scarecrow, "you can have the cheese and olives. I don't like them but my wife always includes them when she makes a packed lunch."

¶ Enemies may sometimes be willing to share the good things of life, but only if they are characters in a fable.

4 THE CARAVAN

A camel that was drinking water from a pool in an oasis was approached by a merchant. "Would you like to join our caravan? We are travelling to the fabled city of Samarkand and we need as many camels as possible. I can promise an interesting journey."

The camel raised his head. "What make is it?"

The merchant frowned. "Pardon?"

"The caravan. What make is it? Does it have its own electricity? How big is it inside? How many wheels does it possess? Will I have a berth to myself or must I share with others?"

The merchant tugged at his pointed beard. "Actually it's not that sort of caravan." And he explained the original meaning of the word to the camel, who rolled his eyes and said:

"What! You expect me to walk all the way to Samarkand and carry your things for you too? No thanks!"

¶ Don't give camels the hump.

5 SOMETHING FISHY

An odd-job man called Tim was in the habit of wandering the land with a fish in a bowl of salt water. The fish was a large flatfish. Tim was willing to do all kinds of work. One day an astronomer asked him to fix his radio telescope. Tim tried hard but had to admit defeat. The next day he went back to try again, but discovered that the radio telescope had already been fixed by another odd-job man who was also

9

called Tim and who also had a fish in a bowl of salt water. "Don't be too upset," said the second Tim to the first. "Just because we have the same name and the same kind of fish doesn't mean we have equal abilities."

¶ There is a Tim and a plaice for everything.

6 BENDING THE KNEE

A group of creatures sat on a wall watching the sunset. The wall had been constructed to stop the sand from the beach blowing over the fields where crops grew. The scene was beautiful.

The hare said, "Let's jump down and dance for joy."

And that's exactly what he did.

The weasel cried, "I'm coming too!" and he also jumped down. So did the fox, cat, monkey, grasshopper and aardvark. They capered in the ruby light and their shadows on the beach were amazingly long. The millipede was scared and remained on the wall.

"It's a long way down," he said nervously.

The hare said, "Don't worry. It won't hurt if you just bend your knees when you land to absorb the impact."

"Bend my knees!" exclaimed the millipede. "But it's almost evening. I don't have all day, you know!"

¶ What has a million legs? One thousand millipedes.

7 BATHTIME FOR MOONS

A crescent moon was feeling tired, so he decided to have a nice dip in the Pacific Ocean. He lay back on his curve and just floated there without a care in the world or a care in the moon.

But an iceberg happened to pass along and when it saw the moon it couldn't believe its eyes, partly because it didn't have any eyes and partly because it had no belief. Yet it was amazed.

"Oh my!" it muttered to itself. "Look at the size of that banana!"

¶ It's easier than you might think to confuse fruit with celestial bodies. How can you be sure the sun isn't just a grapefruit?

8 AN HORRIFIC OUTCOME

A horror writer at a literary convention was bragging about his ability to frighten people. "I am the weaver of nightmares!" he declared. "I am the lurker on the threshold of the night lands! I have peered into the abyss of ultimate terror and flinched not at what I saw! I am the monger of visions beyond the ken of mortal man, yea beyond the ken and also beyond the keith and malcolm. I am the envoy of the amorphous force that dwells in the spaces between the stars and toys with the destiny of mortals in the same way an overwrought metaphor toys with a grandiose comparison. I am the messenger of morbid menace!"

The person he addressed these words to was embarrassed and tried to change the topic of conversation by asking, "Are you planning on going anywhere nice for your summer holidays? Somewhere abroad, maybe? Flights are very cheap at the moment."

But the horror writer suddenly turned pale and began trembling. "Oh no! I can't do that. I'm scared of flying!"

¶ Writers are full of crap.

9 CIRCUIT TRAINING

The inherent processes of an electronic circuit began grumbling to each other. "Why are you always so negative?" Input demanded of Feedback, who responded with the words, "It's just my destiny, I can't help it." But Output wasn't ready to accept that explanation and sniffed, "It's because he's a control-freak, that's why!"

¶ A bad process always blames its definition.

10 A WOBBLY DISPUTE

A pair of buttocks was arguing with a pair of breasts. "Everyone knows that the capital of Australia is Melbourne," insisted the buttocks. "No, it's not," snapped the breasts. "Yes it is!" cried the buttocks, growing heated. "I tell you that it isn't," retorted the breasts. "Then," growled the buttocks, "it must be Sydney instead." "That's also wrong," said the breasts. "How can that be?" demanded the buttocks.

"You don't know everything about geography," sneered the breasts. "You don't seriously expect me to believe that the capital of Australia is Adelaide?" gasped the buttocks. "No, I don't, because that's not right either," said the breasts. "I hate you," said the buttocks. "Bugger off," said the breasts.

¶ Some fables, like this one, are pointless and stupid.

11 TELLING THE TELLERS

A duck, a melon and an anecdote were travelling on a ship. "Let's tell stories to pass the time!" the duck suggested. The melon was enthusiastic and rolled around excitedly while the duck went first. "Once upon a time there was a pond that had never seen its own reflection. One day a young lady walked past and dropped her mirror in the water. When the pond saw what it looked like, it was very upset. 'I'm so soft!' it groaned. 'Why can't I be hard like a boulder?' The months passed and the season changed and in the depths of winter the pond froze solid. 'Woe is me!' it lamented. 'I got what I wanted, but now skaters scar me with the sharp blades on their boots. I can't wait to thaw out again!'"

The melon was very impressed with this fable and tried hard to relate one of equal worth. "In a land far away lived a doorknob. It thought that everybody loved it, because people kept caressing it. 'I'm so popular that I ought to be the president of the republic I dwell in,' it said to itself. So it detached itself from the door and went to the presidential palace to usurp

13

the incumbent ruler. But the true president merely glanced at it and said, 'My lavatory door is lacking a knob. This one will do fine!' And so the doorknob became covered with germs from unwashed hands and realised that it would never be loved again."

Now it was the anecdote's turn. But it had been busy drilling a hole in the bottom of the ship. As they began to drown it said, "Why should I *tell* a story? Don't you know who I am?"

¶ When ability goes unrecognised, don't be too surprised if it decides to get up to mischief undetected.

12 THE HIPPY BEACH

There was a cloud with alternative leanings who decided to drop out of the expected weather patterns, tune in to the vibe of the cosmos and turn on his higher consciousness; so he left his familiar pack of cumulus colleagues and headed for a beach he had been told about where he might expect to find the things he was seeking.

But when he arrived, the beach was just like a desert and it wasn't as nice as the cloud had been led to believe. He looked about rather critically and finally he shouted, "Call this a hippy beach? Everything about it is utterly dismal and pointless. There's no spiritual atmosphere at all. Come to think of it, where's the tide?"

A grain of sand answered, "Far out, man."

¶ So it was a hippy beach after all.

Drifting along in space, a cosmic spider was explaining to a galactic moth how it caught supper for itself. "First I make a web and then if I wait long enough I always catch something edible."

The moth was intrigued. "What's your favourite food?"

"Planets," answered the spider.

"Do you catch many of those, I wonder?"

The spider nodded. "So many that I can't eat them all, so I leave some in storage for a rainy day. We don't get many rainy days in outer space, but you know what I mean. Anyway, the funny thing is that some of these planets are infested with parasites."

"Civilisations, you mean?" queried the moth.

"Exactly. And the inhabitants of those civilisations often think that my webs are lines of latitude and longitude. They sometimes use the separate strands for navigational purposes."

"That's hilarious!" chuckled the moth.

"Isn't it?" agreed the spider.

The moth said, "Well, it was nice talking to you, but I've got work to do now. I have to circle that star over there a hundred times and then try to extinguish it by flying into it."

"Good luck. Take care," said the spider.

¶ Four legs good, two legs bad, eight legs weird.

14 THE WHEELS OF CHANCE

A knife and book were so dismayed at the way they were treated that they decided to escape together, so the knife slid out of the kitchen drawer one evening and went to join the book, who had fluttered down from his shelf and was waiting for him at the back door.

"We'll steal the master's bicycle and make a rapid getaway!" suggested the book. The knife readily agreed to this, so they unlocked the garage and took the bicycle, and soon they were racing down the road away from the house. But they were still anxious that the owner of the bicycle might be running after them on foot.

"Pedal faster!" urged the knife.

"I can't," replied the book, "because I don't have legs."

"Neither do I," said the knife.

Now they were freewheeling down a steep hill, accelerating towards a brick wall at the bottom. "Put the brakes on!" cried the book. And he shut his covers tightly and trembled.

"I can't," squeaked the knife, "because I don't have hands."

"Neither do I," said the book.

"I've learned a valuable lesson today," sadly sighed the knife, "because even though you are a much-reprinted textbook on Bicycle Maintenance, you don't actually know anything about the day-to-day operation of these popular machines. And now it seems we are going to be mangled beyond recognition in a dreadful collision!"

And so they were. But the wall just smiled.

¶ This fable is a warning to pure theorists to get their hands dirty with some practical work. If they refuse to do so, it is almost certain they will eventually get their faces bashed in.

15 BANDIT AND THE BRIDGE

There was a badger called Bandit who built a bridge across a raging river and charged travellers a small sum to cross safely over. One day a woolly mammoth wanted to cross the bridge.

"I must forbid you to make the attempt," said Bandit, "because you are far too heavy for such a structure." The mammoth grew highly annoyed at this refusal and barged past without paying the fee. But when he was only halfway across, the bridge collapsed.

"Alas, I was a fool!" lamented the mammoth as the current carried him off to a waterfall. "This badger's advice would have enabled me not only to save my life but my finances too."

"That's not quite right," Bandit called after him, "because I would have been more than happy to receive your crossing fee even if you had made a detour. I'm not a charity! As it happens, I plan to sue your descendants for the full cost of repairing my bridge and for loss of earnings, plus the mental stress this incident caused me."

¶ Breaking a badger's bridge is basically bad.

16 HOLIDAY SUN

The sun needed a holiday, so it decided to travel to a place it had never been before. But the fiery ball that suddenly appeared in the sky terrified the people who lived there. They thought it must be an unlucky omen or even a foreigner. "Go back to where you came!" they screamed. "There's no room for the likes of you in Wales!"

¶ Simpletons often shun the unexpected.

17 THE CONDEMNED MAN

A prisoner was found guilty of murder and sentenced to be executed by beheading at dawn the following day. He bitterly contested this judgment with the words, "I performed that crime more than thirty years ago. Since then, my personality has changed; so has my entire body, and in fact there isn't a single molecule inside me now that is the same as when the victim was strangled. I'm a completely different individual from the fellow who performed the deed. If I am decapitated tomorrow morning, you will be guilty of taking the life of an innocent man. How will the executioner live with his conscience after such an injustice?"

"His conscience will bother him a lot, if what you say is true," replied the judge, "and for many days and weeks he will feel acute anguish. But as more time passes, his personality will change and the molecules inside his body will be replaced one by one until he becomes a completely new individual, and that future individual can't possibly be held responsible for hacking off your head, so don't worry!"

¶ When smug people meet, the smuggest will prevail.

18 NOT A PATCH

A cumulus cloud kept rushing through the atmosphere, north, south, east and west; it never stopped for a moment. A sentient hot-air balloon asked if it had lost something. "I can't think of any other reason why you should be hurrying through the sky like that."

"I'm looking for a patch of sunlight on the ground," said the cumulus cloud, "because I have been told they are worth seeing, but whenever I learn that one has appeared somewhere, it always vanishes by the time I arrive at the designated location. All I get to see is a shadow that happens to be precisely the same shape as me."

"That's a weird coincidence," said the hot-air balloon. "The same thing happens to me but on a smaller scale."

¶ Things often get in their own way.

19 THE TEA AND THE CAKE

A lonely cake saw some biscuits having fun and pined to join them. "I wish I was a biscuit!" it lamented to itself. Finally it hatched a plan to disguise itself as a biscuit and join them by stealth. This plan worked well until the time came for the biscuits to be dunked in a large mug of milky tea by an old woman. Casting off its disguise, the cake cried, "A dip in that anaemic brew isn't *my* cup of tea."

¶ Cakes and biscuits aren't the same, not even for tax purposes.

20 DRINKING PARTNERS

A gnome and a Viking were playing croquet on the lawn. The gnome hit the ball so hard that it rolled over the horizon and was gone. "I'll go and fetch it!" he announced. "Be careful," warned the Viking, "for it is said that no one who journeys over that horizon has ever returned and I'd like you to come back safely, not because I'm sentimental but because I want to finish this game. I'm beating you."

The gnome went off and after a long journey beyond the horizon was delighted to find himself in a magic land where all the rocks were edible and the lakes were alcoholic beverages. While bending down to sip from a deep pool of fermented honey, he fell in and began to drown. "Help! I'm sinking in a bottomless pond of mead!"

The Viking had secretly followed the gnome and perceived his plight. Immediately he jumped into the pool. "Don't struggle," he said, "I'll drink you out!" And he began gulping down the potent liquid. The gnome was touched by his comrade's bravery, but the Viking dismissed his gratitude with the words, "It's my (hic!) pleasure."

¶ A friend in mead is a friend indeed.

21 SWEET TALK

A chimp, a scarf and a hive were debating among themselves which of them had the most beautiful life. "I can peel bananas with my feet," said the chimp, "and that's one of the most beautiful things anyone can ever hope to do." But the scarf wasn't intimidated in the slightest and shouted, "I get thrown around necks and often my ends just dangle down, but in a strong wind they stick out horizontally; how can any conceivable thing be more beautiful than that?" But the hive laughed and said, "Flying insects live inside me and fill me with honey."

¶ Beauty is in the eye of the bee holder.

22 THE ROBOT TAILOR

Long after mankind had been wiped from the face of the planet, thanks to a combination of environmental and technological factors, the robots that now controlled everything discovered they weren't as happy as they ought to be. They realised that they missed the company of organic men and women. So they attempted to recreate the human race by experimenting in their laboratories with genetic material.

Unfortunately none of the experiments were successful. One morning, a robot associated with one of the most important labs was gliding along an elevated walkway when he came upon another robot that was sewing rags together into shirts, trousers and coats. "What are you doing, wasting time with those scraps?" the first robot cried.

The second robot didn't stop working but merely rasped, "I read in an old book that *clothes maketh the man*, so it occurred to me that if I make the clothes first, then they can do the rest."

¶ Only a fool takes seriously the advice of proverbs.

23 THE CLOCKWORK DRAGON

A clockwork dragon lived in the attic of a shop where a watchmaker sold chronometers and other precision timepieces. Often he came downstairs to keep the watchmaker company.

Sometimes, when the watchmaker went out to visit friends, the dragon was left in charge all by himself. He took orders, prepared invoices, filled out tax returns and other such tasks.

Most customers were tolerant of the presence of the dragon in the shop but every so often an awkward person would enter and say, "It's not right for dragons or other mythical beings to reside on business premises. You ought to be based in a remote cave."

"This shop is quite cavelike," answered the dragon.

"That's not the point," the awkward customer would continue. "What if a damsel with a broken wristwatch came in? Would you chain her up or devour her? You simply aren't safe."

"I don't eat people. I'm a clockwork dragon. I get all my energy from a mainspring coiled up tight inside me."

One day a customer leaned across the counter and began twisting the key on the dragon's back. "Clockwork dragons are even more dangerous than the normal kind," he said. "Not only do they eat damsels in a matter of *minutes*, but they always come back for *seconds*."

"Hey!" responded the dragon. "Are you winding me up?"

¶ Puff the magic dragon. You do know how to do that, don't you? Just put your lips together and blow.

24 A PAIR OF SURFERS

There was an ocean made of hands. Two surfers decided it would be fun to paddle out and ride the waves back to shore, so they drove all night to reach the location, but when they stood on the beach and looked out they soon changed their minds. "Those aren't waves. The hands aren't waving at all. They are giving us the finger!"

¶ Never expect a sea of hands to be polite to you.

25 THE GIANT WALKING SKELETON

A giant walking skeleton shook its head and said, "My life is a hard one. All day long I have been balancing these bags full of arrows on the vertebrae of my exposed spine; and now a bunch of desert chieftains have set up home in my hollow left femur."

"I know a song about that," said a passing hippogriff.

"Sing it then," suggested the skeleton.

"Quivers down my backbone… I've got the sheiks in my thigh-bone," crooned the hippogriff.

¶ The old ones are the best, allegedly.

26 THE ADDICT

A crack addict was huddled in the doorway of a condemned house in the centre of a city where criminals were more common than flies. Half in the shadows, half in the inhuman glare of the damaged sodium light, he drew his filthy blanket tighter around his thin shoulders and shivered. His eyes bulged and in his ears throbbed the awful sounds of men beating up wives and psychopaths torturing small animals.

A philanthropist passed and stopped and said to the addict, "I'm a rich eccentric and can give you enough money to get yourself back on your feet and out of this truly dreadful place and you don't have to do anything sordid in return. What do you say to that?"

"No thanks," replied the addict.

The philanthropist was amazed but decided to try again. "I see you are too proud to accept charity. In that case I can give you advice on how to become self-employed and earn your own money. The end result will be the same and your life will improve."

"I'm not interested," insisted the addict.

The philanthropist was flabbergasted by this response. "But surely you don't intend to remain there forever?"

The addict shook his head and answered:

"Not forever, no. But I don't want to change my situation. I'm waiting to be used as a character in a novel by one of those modern writers who write a style of fiction called *miserablism* that feeds on the bad things of modern urban life. I think they represent my best opportunity."

¶ Misery loves a publishing company.

27 A LOT OF BOTTLE

A bottle of beer was revising for a maths exam. It was a bottle of Abbaye de Leffe (6.6% ABV) and it was having trouble understanding the way in which Pascal's Triangle determines the coefficients that arise in binomial expansions. A mouse who happened to be watching laughed and said, "You'll never get to grips with that problem." The bottle of beer was annoyed and demanded, "Why not?" The mouse laughed even louder and said, "Because you're a *blonde* beer!"

¶ Stick to what you know best.

28 A SPIKY ELECTION

The hedgehogs got together and decided to create a republic to safeguard their rights. They marked out a suitable territory, created a set of laws and even designed a flag. The next step was to elect a president. Four of the wisest, bravest and most ambitious hedgehogs shuffled forward to offer themselves as candidates for the position.

During the election campaign, the first hedgehog adopted 'I can juggle slugs' as his motto and he won 9% of the vote. The second hedgehog's motto was 'Free apples for all' and he won 17% of the vote. The third hedgehog preferred 'Dogs to be exiled to the moon' and he won 23% of the vote. But the fourth hedgehog's motto was simply 'I know everything about everything' and he won a majority.

When the results were announced and it became clear that the fourth hedgehog had won 51% of the vote, the three losers managed to repress their anger and congratulate him, but they couldn't resist saying, "Your campaign slogan was very presumptuous!"

"Of course it was!" replied the new president of the hedgehog republic with a broad smile. "And that's how I won. But don't worry; you will get your turn at this job too. One should always presume. If one presumes, one makes a PRES out of U and ME…"

¶ A political hedgehog is about as much use as an astronomical cat.

29 THE BRAIN OF MÖBIUS

There was a Möbius Strip who resented the fact he only had one side and one edge. "Fancy being a two-dimensional entity in a three-dimensional universe!" he grumbled. "It's very unfair."

He was so upset by his condition that he begged a passing scissors to snip him in half. The scissors wanted to decline, but the Möbius Strip was determined. "Very well, here we go!"

The blades clashed together, severing fibres.

The Möbius Strip straightened himself with pleasure. "Now I'm the same as any length of normal fabric!"

A few weeks later he was visited by a Klein Bottle who said, "How disappointing! I was planning to invite you to join an influential society of unusual shapes and solids, but I see that you are nothing more than a glorified ribbon. What's more, someone or something has cut your brain in half. So you're no use at all to me!"

¶ If you have a twisted personality, accept and enjoy it.

30 JAM ON AN AARDVARK'S NOSE

A gorilla was bored and made a private vow that he would do something that nobody else had ever done before, so he travelled for many months until he came across an aardvark asleep in the shade of a tree. "Sorry for waking you," said the gorilla, "but I'm wondering if you can do me a favour?" The aardvark responded sleepily, "What's that, my hairy friend from faraway?" The gorilla explained, "Just stay where you are while I spread some apricot jam on your nose."

The aardvark sighed. "You didn't have to wake me up to make that request! You could have just gone ahead and spread the jam when I was sleeping and I probably wouldn't have noticed." The gorilla accepted this rebuke meekly and opened the jam jar.

When the nose was completely covered in jam, the gorilla stood back to examine his work. "Are you satisfied?" asked the aardvark. "Yes, it's not bad," said the gorilla. "Did you want anything else?" questioned the aardvark. "No, that's sufficient. I'll go home now. Nice to meet you and thanks for this opportunity. Goodbye!"

And the gorilla began the journey back home, but when he arrived he found that his female had run off with an ocarina.

¶ Not everything that has never been done before is worth doing.

31 MISSED OPPORTUNITY

A hot-air balloon was drifting over a landscape when it happened to gaze down at a peculiar creature sitting on the summit of a hill. "What on earth are you?" the balloon wondered. "I'm the largest gastropod in the world," came the reply. "What's a gastropod?" asked the balloon. "I don't actually know," admitted the entity. "Why not find out?" pressed the balloon. "Is it important?" the gastropod queried. "Yes," nodded the

28

balloon, "because I want to invite you to dinner, but until I know what you are I can't issue a formal invitation. Isn't that obvious?"

"Maybe it is, but I can't oblige," said the gastropod, "because I don't own a dictionary." "But I do!" the balloon shouted gleefully. "Look the word up then," the gastropod suggested. "I'm a balloon and don't possess hands to turn the pages," sighed the balloon, "but I can throw it down and you can find the word for both of us!"

The gastropod was just about to dissuade the balloon from taking this course of action when the book came plummeting down, landing nearby. So it looked up the word and recited aloud for the benefit of the balloon, "A mollusc with a large flattened foot."

But the balloon was rising rapidly. The large dictionary had acted like jettisoned ballast and with less weight to keep its altitude low the balloon was soon in the stratosphere. "Sorry!"

"Maybe next time," said the gastropod philosophically.

¶ If you wait until the parameters of a potential new friend are rigidly defined you may never get to eat dinner with them.

32 DON'T SHOOT THE MESSENGER

A king once ordered a messenger to deliver a sealed envelope to another king. The messenger set off on the dangerous journey and he was never tempted to open the envelope and read the message within. After months of hard travelling, he finally reached the palace of the second king, who opened the envelope in front of him and read the letter with a frown that grew deeper and deeper. Finally he reached for a loaded blunderbuss and pointed it at the messenger's head.

"Clearly you have received some bad news," said the messenger, "but I'm not responsible for what has happened, so don't shoot the messenger! I simply completed my given task."

Silently, but with a grim expression, the king handed the letter to the messenger, who began sweating as he read it. The message said simply, "Please shoot the messenger who delivers this to you." The king pulled the trigger of the gun and it went off.

¶ Go on, shoot the messenger!

33 THE SKINT SKUNK

There was once a skunk that had no money. He was completely out of cash and he didn't own any property either. When he was at his wits' end he appealed to the author of this fable.

"Why the hell did you make me so poor?" he cried.

The author of this fable — who happens to be me — heard his plea and reluctantly entered the text. "I needed a skint skunk for a fable I'm writing and you're the one," I said.

"Does your fable have a worthwhile message?"

I shrugged my shoulders. "No idea. I just started writing it without any thoughts about where it might lead."

"Then why put me in it? You could have used anyone!"

"That's true," I admitted, "but I like the alliteration of the words *skint skunk* and that's how it happened that you came into existence. That really was my entire motive, nothing more."

"You irresponsible dullard!" bellowed the skunk.

"In return for that insult," I responded with indignation, "I'm going to terminate your fable this very mo—"

¶ Fabulists are no nicer than anyone else.

34 THE SHORTEST MONTH

February is the shortest month of the year, as everyone knows, and this simple fact made it feel humiliated, just like Napoleon. It felt it had to compensate for its shortness by conquering its neighbours, so one day it unexpectedly invaded March and January, and after fierce fighting it took them over; then it embarked on a campaign to expand its empire and take over the entire year, which it soon did.

But it fell in love with June and they got married and had a child. The child was named *Junuary*, because it had inherited roughly equal qualities from both parents. But there was no room for it in the calendar. Emperor February insisted that it should be inserted between April and May. That's what happened, but as a consequence the scheme of the year was messed up and nobody knew what date it was.

Even the Earth got confused as it orbited the sun and forgot to turn the bend at the right time and went shooting off into interstellar space, where it is still wandering aimlessly right now.

¶ Be satisfied with the days you are given.

35 ABOVE HIS STATION

A philosopher was travelling on a train from Swansea to Tenby. It was a nice journey, but he wasn't happy because his mind was a blank. It was his official job to keep having ideas, but not a single new one had come to him for ages. When he reached his destination he got out of the train with the words, "This is my station."

As he stood on the platform, he wondered if jumping into the air might help. So he made a pole from the branch of a tree and pole-vaulted over the railway tracks. As he reached the highest point of his immense jump, a new idea finally came to him.

His delight was short lived. On the opposite platform a hippopotamus was waiting for its own train and it happened to be yawning at that exact moment, maybe because it was tired or practicing for a competition. The philosopher landed in its mouth and vanished down its throat and into its stomach, never to be seen again.

¶ Don't get ideas above your station.

36 THE ROOK AND THE JACKDAW

A crow that had recently eaten cheese and olives with a scarecrow was interested in unusual friendships. He saw a rook and a jackdaw together in a field and said, "Excuse me, but I'm curious to know why rooks and jackdaws always seem to get on so well. You never mix with ravens or magpies or jays or any other corvid."

"Rooks and jackdaws are natural allies," said the jackdaw.

"Yes, but why?" persisted the crow.

"Because we have a shared interest in chess," said the rook.

The crow was amazed. "Really?"

"Yes, it's true," confirmed the jackdaw, "but you won't see us with a board and we use random objects for pieces. For instance, this twig is the white king and this leaf is the queen."

"What are the pawns?" asked the crow.

"These little stones here."

"What about the bishops and the knights?"

"Worms and mushrooms."

"And the piece that is shaped like a castle? I can't remember its proper name. What do you use for that?"

"I play that part myself," said the rook.

¶ Don't be mean to birds, they are highly intelligent.

37 THE TWEED JACKET

There was a tweed jacket that thought it was the most stylish item of clothing in the wardrobe. "I'm bound to win all the awards this year," it said to itself. But when the time came to announce the winner of the best-dressed entity, the main prize went to a bird. The tweed jacket got angry and began trying to bully the bird. "The competition was rigged! I am the best!" it squeaked. It got so angry that it burst into flames and turned to ashes that blew away on the winds of oblivion.

¶ Tweed is an unfashionable fabric for good reason.

38 RECURSION

A lion overheard the Sun and Moon talking about recursion, but because he didn't understand the meaning of the word he rushed back to his lair to consult a dictionary.

Although he had difficulty turning the pages with his paws, he located the word successfully but the definition confused him. Under 'Recursion' were the words: *Another name for 'Recursion'*. The lion shook his head at this, shut the book and opened it again in order to look up the new word. But under 'Recursion' were the words: *Another name for 'Recursion'*. The lion was none the wiser, so it closed the book again, opened it a third time and looked up the word 'Recursion'. But still it found the words: *Another name for 'Recursion'*.

At this point, the lion began to suspect a trick. So he left his lair and went to visit a friend, a giant gastropod who also owned a dictionary. The gastropod was proud of his dictionary, which he claimed had been given to him by a sentient hot-air balloon.

"I nearly got stuck in a loop," explained the lion, "but I saw the trap in time; and that's probably why I'm the king of the beasts. Let me use your dictionary, if you have no objection."

"Certainly. Here you are," said the gastropod helpfully.

The lion opened the book and looked up the word 'Recursion'. At first he was pleased to encounter a definition different from the one in his own dictionary, but ultimately it was no less baffling. Under 'Recursion' were the words: *A lion overheard the Sun and Moon talking about recursion, but because he didn't understand the meaning of the word he rushed back to his lair to consult a dictionary...*

¶ I could go on like this all day, but that would be wrong.

39 THE LIBRARIAN

There was a man by the name of Gwilym who had the loudest voice in the world. It was so loud that when he spoke foghorns broke or fled. So he decided to become a librarian. Never let it be said that the quiet ones are the strangest of all! Gwilym wore a top hat and carried a pocket watch even though he lived in the 21st Century.

A foghorn that was braver than others of his kind went to pay Gwilym a visit at work on the pretext of borrowing a book on acoustics. When he passed Gwilym's desk, the foghorn couldn't resist a gibe, saying, "When you speak I can hear you ten miles away!"

"People have told me that before," said Gwilym.

"In fact," corrected the foghorn, "I can hear you fifty miles away."

"I don't doubt it," replied Gwilym.

The foghorn said, "I'm not being perfectly candid. When you speak I can hear you two hundred miles away."

"Tell me something new," sighed Gwilym.

The foghorn began to grow exasperated. "Look here, I might as well be honest and say that when you speak in a whisper I can hear you clearly more than one thousand miles away!"

"Yes, yes, that doesn't surprise me in the least!"

The foghorn made one final attempt to insult the librarian. "You ought to know the full truth of the matter. Even when you just move your lips silently, I can hear you at a distance of 24,000 miles. How about that? I bet nobody ever told you that before?"

"True," concurred Gwilym, then he leaned forward and added, "but that's much less impressive; and in fact it suggests you might be hard of hearing. You see, I'm standing at that exact distance from you right now. It's the circumference of the Earth!"

The foghorn left the library in shame. It forgot to bring the borrowed book back in time and was fined.

¶ Never forget that planets are round.

40 TRUNKS

An elephant that was fond of practical jokes dialled a random number on the telephone. "Hello?" said a distant voice at the other end. "This is a trunk call!" chortled the elephant. Then it made a trumpeting noise into the receiver and waited for the response.

But the voice on the other end failed to see the joke.

"Good. I'm glad it's a trunk call," it said, "because I'm a tree and thus am in possession of a trunk. Therefore your call must certainly be suitable for me. What do you wish to say?"

The elephant grew annoyed. "You spoiled my jest, even though it was a rather corny one. I am offended by your attitude. I hereby challenge you to a duel! Do you accept or refuse?"

"I accept, of course! I have fought many duels."

"Tomorrow then!" roared the elephant. "Where shall we meet?"

"I'm not really in the habit of going far. I'm sessile, you see," answered the tree. "You'll have to come to me."

"Fine. I'll catch the early train," said the elephant.

"It's a long way," said the tree.

"I don't mind distance. I'm a seasoned traveller."

"Don't forget to pack your trunk."

¶ Corniness is as corniness does; and yet practical jokers will always be superior to the theoretical kind.

41 SILLY GOOSE

A meteorite skimmed low over a pond. "Duck!" cried a heron. All the birds dived under the water except one, who was grazed painfully by the passing of the fiery space stone. "Why didn't you warn me?" it shouted at the heron. "But I did!" came the response. "No, you didn't," insisted the wounded bird. "I shouted out 'Duck'," said the heron. "Yes indeed," was the retort to this, "but I'm a goose."

¶ What's good for the meteorite is good for the comet.

42 THE ROCK POOL

There was a rock pool that fell in love with a wave. As the sun began to set in the west, he said to her, "You are so beautiful and frothy. Why not come a bit closer and break over me?"

But the wave recoiled at his suggestion. "No thanks!" And she made sure she avoided him until the tide turned and it was time for her to leave the beach behind and return to deeper waters. The rock pool was hurt and called after her, "What's the problem?"

"You have crabs," she said without hesitation.

¶ In amorous matters, blunt honesty is the sharpest weapon.

43 THE WINDMILL

A windmill that was fixed to its base liked to daydream about changing his career. Because he couldn't move, his first name was Sessile; because he had two tiny windows for eyes, his middle name was Beady; because he was a windmill his surname was Mill.

"I'm fed up with turning in the wind all day," he sighed.

A fox and carrot happened to be passing and they asked him, "If that's the case, what would you rather be?"

"A film director," came the reply.

The fox was highly amused. "But do you know anything at all about the movie business? It's a very competitive field. And how would you pay your actors and finance your projects?"

"With bread. I make plenty of it," said Sessile Beady Mill.

"Fair enough," conceded the carrot.

¶ It's acceptable to be corny if the end result is dough.

44 THE ICE HARLOT

Up in the far north, above the Arctic Circle, there was a harlot who lived in a brothel made from icicles. The icicles were woven together like poles of bamboo and it was a very clever and original construction, if you enjoy that kind of thing. Personally I don't.

An explorer who didn't really like the cold very much once visited the harlot. He had made the wrong career choice when he was younger and that's why he was an explorer instead of something else. Mind you, I don't think he would have been much good at *any* sort of job. Just my opinion, take or leave it. Anyway, he engaged the harlot for her services, but only managed to endure ten minutes of it.

"I was feeling so cold I came here to get myself warmed up," he cried as he shivered without any clothes on.

"Warmed up? What a perfectly bizarre notion!"

"You're a prostitute, aren't you?"

She shook her head. "No, I'm a *frostytute*. I'm made of ice crystals that just happened to form in the shape of a woman. If you agree, we can wait a few more minutes and then try again."

"Snow thanks," said the explorer as he hurried out.

¶ He got lost on the way home, incidentally.

45 TWO CHIVES

Two chives that were growing in a pot had an argument. They decided to settle their dispute by fighting each other. Despite the fact they were the smallest species of onion, they managed to do a lot of damage and before long they were both badly injured.

"This is extremely silly," said the first chive.

"I agree," said the second chive. "Why don't we settle the matter some other way? For instance, we should roll this dice. I'll go first and you can go second. Highest number wins!"

"I believe that 'die' is the singular of dice," said the first chive.

"I stand corrected," said the second chive sardonically. Then he rolled the die and squinted to see the result.

"It's a one!" chortled the first chive.

"Now it's your turn," said the second chive unhappily.

The first chive also rolled the dice. But the result was the same. "It's another one! It's a draw!" he gasped.

The second chive peered closer and frowned.

"Wait a moment! This die has been interfered with... Every face has the number one inscribed on it..."

¶ When two chives go to war, a point is all that they can score.

46 THE FABLE WITH A MORAL LONGER THAN ITS TEXT

There was once a fable with a moral longer than its text. But it slipped and fell over the edge of a cliff.

¶ This fable is metafictional, in the sense that it refers to itself, partly for simple entertainment purposes, partly in an attempt to question the very nature of fables, which is an ironic function. When walking on cliff tops it's always best not to wander too close to the edge. Metafiction is feared by traditional literary critics, who deride it and pretend it doesn't exist. If you look before you leap, make certain that you are looking in the right direction; there's no point looking south if you are leaping north, unless your vision stretches right around the world.

47 GET YOUR INSULTS RIGHT!

There was a hare that lived on a scalp. The scalp belonged to an odd-job man called Tim who kept a fish in a bowl of water. The fish was in the habit of mocking the hare. "Hey, big ears!"

The hare ignored the insults and declined to reply.

"Hey, big ears!" persisted the fish.

But the ears on the side of Tim's head thought the fish was referring to them. Distraught by the constant taunting, they decided to leave and find another skull to attach themselves to.

Tim was furious when he discovered what had happened. "How can I hear anything without ears?" he cried.

"I'm sure you'll manage," answered the fish.

"What did you say?" asked Tim.

The hare had no desire to live on the scalp of a deaf man, so it jumped right off and went hitchhiking instead.

¶ Keep your hare on!

48 LUMP IN THE THROAT

A carnivorous dinosaur belonging to a hitherto unknown species that had survived into the 21st Century was showing off to his female by eating a group of villagers without chewing them. First he ate the chief and his six wives; next he swallowed seven or eight tribal elders whole; and then he devoured the local medicine man.

Finally he attempted to consume a strange white fellow with a peculiar object hanging from a strap around his neck. This object clicked as it got wedged in the greedy dinosaur's gullet together with the man who wore it. The dinosaur coughed and spluttered but couldn't spit the morsel out; and he began to breathe with difficulty.

The swallowed fellow wailed, "Help! I'm a Dutch tourist and not used to being eaten by monsters! I've got some great photos though! Perhaps I can sell them to *National Geographic*?"

"Dutch? Oh dear!" lamented the female dinosaur. She turned to her mate and said, "It seems you've got a foreign object stuck in your throat. I'd better take you along to the A&E department of the local hospital. I hope they are willing to treat you."

"What does A&E stand for?" wheezed the male dinosaur.

"Archaic and Extinct," came the reply.

¶ Don't wolf your food, even if you are much bigger and fiercer than a wolf. I'm assuming that's what the moral is; I might be wrong.

49 METROPOLIS

A robot that lived in the future had an air-car that he liked to fly around his hometown on weekends. He was so successful at his job, which had something to do with magnets, that he was promoted and told to relocate to a bigger office in a bigger city. In fact he was despatched to the capital of the robot world, where the headquarters of his organisation was based. He agreed to do this and moved home.

In the capital city he worked hard and his colleagues were pleased by his performance, but when the week was over and all the employees went home for the weekend, disaster struck! The robot flew his air-car into the side of a building and he was utterly destroyed. He had forgotten that the capital city was constructed from transparent building materials. After all, it was supposed to be a futuristic design!

¶ Robots in glass cities shouldn't fly cars.

50 THE TARNISHED RULE

A clever sage once learned everything there was to know about religion, philosophy and ethics. He said, "I've found one thing that these faiths and systems of thought have in common."

A traveller who was passing stopped and answered, "That's amazing. You mean you've distilled the wisdom of the ages into a single truth that you can spread among all the nations?"

"Yep," nodded the sage.

"What is that truth, O guru?" asked the traveller.

"It's called the Golden Rule and it's quite simple really. *Do unto others as you would have done unto you.*"

"Is that all there is to it?" gasped the traveller.

"Indeedy," confirmed the sage.

"Are you absolutely certain about this?" persisted the traveller.

"I am," said the sage confidently.

"So if I do unto others as I would have done unto me I'll be the holiest sort of man? Is that really true?"

"Sure. And a blessing on your effort," said the sage.

The traveller went to a shop and bought a long whip. Then he started lashing everybody on the buttocks. Soon they were all howling, bleeding and jumping into ponds to cool down.

"What are you doing?" screeched the sage.

"I'm merely doing unto others what I would have done unto me," came the reply. "I'm a masochist, you see…"

¶ That shut the sage up, the smug git.

51 LOOKING UP

A dictionary once decided to look itself up. So it opened itself, turned to the relevant page and read the entry next to the word 'dictionary'. But a giant gastropod laughed at him.

"Nobody ever looks the word 'dictionary' up in a dictionary! That's a ridiculous thing to do!" he said.

"If it was so stupid, the word wouldn't be in me," cried the dictionary angrily, "and as a matter of fact, it is."

"I also own a dictionary," declared the gastropod.

The dictionary pretended to be impressed. "And do you enjoy looking up things?" And when the gastropod confessed that he did, the dictionary added, "I've got a suggestion for you."

"Something new for me to look up, you mean?"

The dictionary nodded. "Yes!"

"What is it? Tell me!" pleaded the gastropod.

The dictionary said, "See that girl over there? The redhead with the long legs? Go and look up her skirt."

The gastropod did exactly that. Then he came back. The dictionary managed to repress a laugh and asked:

"So what was the definition?"

"I don't know, but it hurt," said the gastropod.

¶ Redheads slap harder than other colours.

52 SHORT BREAK

An old steam-powered robot was dismantled and thrown into a junkyard. His time was up. But three of the parts inside him, a lever, a valve and a gasket, became good friends and decided to go on holiday together. They chose Corfu as a suitable destination.

They packed their bags carefully but instead of leaving the rest of the robot behind, the lever carried the head; the valve looked after the arms and body; the gasket kept the legs safe.

As soon as they arrived, the lever said, "Let's visit the house where the writer Lawrence Durrell lived."

"Is it near here?" asked the valve.

"It's on the northeast coast," replied the lever.

"I'm willing," said the valve.

But now the gasket spoke up. He growled, "Do we have to? I dislike Durrell's overblown literary style."

"If that's going to be your attitude, why the hell did you bother coming on holiday with us?" cried the lever.

"I'm asking that myself," sneered the gasket.

"You're a big pain in the fulcrum!" screamed the lever in anger. It was left to the valve to restore calm.

"Together we are strong; alone we are weak," he said.

But his wise words were wasted…

"I've had enough. This is crap!" roared the gasket.

"I disagree violently," countered the lever. "Corfu is a beautiful island, full of pleasant things to see and do."

"Not the island, you elongated twit!" cried the gasket. "I was referring to the fable. It's the worst one so far!"

And he stamped his way out of the text…

"We can't go anywhere now!" lamented the lever and valve, "because he was the keeper of the lower limbs."

¶ Don't put all your legs in one gasket.

53 THE FOUNTAIN PEN

A ballpoint pen was ashamed of his appearance and wanted to transform himself into a better sort of writing implement, but there was no obvious solution to his dilemma. After all, a leopard can't change its spots and a pen can't change its inkblots. That's how the saying goes. And it is often good to listen to wise sayings.

Having said that, one morning a passing crow told the ballpoint pen about a clever earwig who could make any wish come true. "Any wish at all?" gasped the ballpoint pen.

"Well, not quite," admitted the crow, "because if the wisher asked for something logically impossible — for example, that all circles should become squares but still remain round — then the earwig would have to admit defeat; but in your case I'm sure there will be no problems. Now I'm off to caw elsewhere. Bye!"

"Take care! And thanks for your help."

The ballpoint pen journeyed to the cave where the earwig lived and finally arrived a few weeks later.

He was tired but excited and blurted out his desire to the earwig, who was willing to grant it. "Please transform me into a fountain pen," was the ballpoint's request. "That's my wish."

"Are you sure about this?" asked the earwig.

"I beg your pardon?"

"Are you sure about this?" shouted the earwig, who had a very quiet voice and always had difficulty making himself heard. The ballpoint pen nodded, so the earwig went and consulted one of his books of magic and then he waved his legs in a special manner and puff! there was a cloud of smoke and the ballpoint pen vanished.

In its place stood a gushing public fountain contained within a fenced area. The fountain gurgled, "What's the meaning of this? I feel all wet and slippery. I'm not a writing implement!"

The earwig was bewildered. "Of course not. You're a fountain pen. A small enclosure for fountains. That is what you asked for, isn't it? I hope so, because the spell only works one way."

¶ Be careful what you ask for, you might get a cliché; or even more drastically, you might not.

54 THE STONE DOG

A stone dog had a chip on its shoulder. "Don't you want salt and vinegar with that chip?" asked a passing scruff.

"I've never had the chance," said the stone dog.

The scruff replied, "But I have some with me. I can spare a pinch and a splash if you really want them."

The stone dog blinked at these offerings.

"That's not the kind of salt and vinegar I like! I only want sea salt and balsamic vinegar. I'm so unhappy!"

"Would you feel better if I gave you a hug?" asked the scruff.

"Maybe, maybe not," said the stone dog.

"Let me try!" suggested the scruff, and he jumped up next to the stone dog and hugged him with platonic affection. The stone dog was forced to admit that he did in fact feel less sad.

"More fool you!" chortled the scruff as he devoured the chip.

¶ Keep your chips safe from scruffs.

55 APPEARANCE OF THE REALM

A strange face materialised above the bed of a weasel. "What the heck are you?" muttered the trembling weasel.

"An unexplained appearance," came the answer.

"Is that like a ghost?"

"Yes. Sort of."

"Well, what do you want?" asked the weasel.

"I need to borrow some cash."

"Whatever for?"

The appearance sighed sadly and said, "I'm not any old appearance but an appearance of the realm, which is the most significant kind. I lost my bulging wallet in a strong current."

"Was that a current of water or a current of air?"

"Neither. A landslide of dried grapes."

The weasel was sympathetic. "Look, I only have £35,000 on me at the present time. Is that sufficient?"

The appearance nodded. "Yes, I think so."

The weasel handed the money over. "When will you pay me back?"

"Tomorrow," said the appearance.

Then he dematerialised, leaving the weasel much poorer. "I think I've been tricked," said the weasel to himself.

And it was true. He had. The appearance never returned. And when the weasel checked on Wikipedia, he learned that there was no such thing as an 'appearance of the realm'.

¶ Appearances can be deceptive.

56 TOO MANY CHARACTERS

A pig, a waffle, a box, a chump, a resentment, a caterpillar, a gift, a loom, a cuttlefish, an aurora borealis, a duvet, a chair, a sunken continent, a cup that runneth over, an ancient paradox, a snivel, a bone, a toothless cog, a piecrust, a passionate kiss, an aching thigh, a broken window, a phantom, a cat, a bathtub, a chimney clogged with twigs, a forced laugh, a chewed pencil, a beetroot stain, a vague feeling, a hovercraft, an argument, a dog, an example of jargon, a butterfly, a solecism, a grotesque fiend, a coconut shy, a confident papaya and a thousand other things had gathered together in a restaurant for a celebratory meal.

The waiter came over to their table and shook his head.

"It's off, I'm afraid," he told them.

"But that's nonsense! We haven't ordered yet!"

The waiter smiled and said, "I didn't mean the food, I meant the moral. There's no way you'll make a decent fable out of *this* situation. There are far too many characters in the story."

¶ Don't multiply fictional protagonists beyond necessity.

57 A QUICK DRINK

Three friends went into a bar. "I'll have a glass of brandy," said the first friend, who was an old fellow.

"Vodka for me," said the second friend, who was a tomb.

The barman served them efficiently.

Now it was the third friend's turn. He happened to be an egg. "Give me a stiff shot of rum!" he ordered.

The barman shook his head. "Sorry. You're underage."

"What do you mean?" cried the egg.

"You haven't even hatched yet!" pointed out the barman.

"Look here," responded the egg, "I'm much older than my two friends. The old fellow is only ninety-eight years old; the tomb dates merely from 450 BC; but I'm the egg of a dinosaur."

¶ This fable is an *eggsample* of an ironic situation.

58 THE HASHISH PIPE

A hashish pipe developed an aversion to smoking. It didn't like being stuffed with cannabis resin and set on fire and then sucked by the mouth of a human being. It became sad.

A passing crow asked what the trouble was.

After the hashish pipe explained everything, the crow said, "I know of a cunning earwig that might be able to help you. He has books of magic in his cave and he can work spells…"

"Can't you help me instead?"

"I suppose I can," said the crow. "Anyway, I'll pick you up in my beak and carry you off somewhere."

"Be careful, I'm still alight! The hippy who is smoking me just went to get some food from the shop."

"Food, you say? That reminds me. I was given some cheese and olives by a scarecrow. How weird is that!"

"Very, I guess," said the hashish pipe.

The crow swooped down and clutched the stem in his beak. Then into the sky he flew and far away; but some of the smoke went into his lungs and he started to find everything funny.

"Hey, I've got the munchies!" he said. "Maybe I ought to go and look for that generous scarecrow again?"

The hashish pipe was distraught.

"Why did you open your beak to speak? I have slipped out and now I am falling into that pond below…"

"Oops! Sorry about that. I'm really high."

"Of course you're high. You're a bird!" exclaimed the hashish pipe as it fell into the pond and was put out.

¶ Stone the crows!

59 TWO BUDDHISTS

Two Buddhists started arguing one evening after a session of meditation. The first Buddhist said, "I bet any money that I've just reduced my ego by a greater percentage than you!"

"Rubbish!" responded the second Buddhist. "I shrank my own ego by no less than 36% in that session..."

"That's nothing! I reduced mine by 42%, you sissy!"

They began fighting with fists.

"I bet any money I'm more compassionate than you!"

"Take that! I'm the gentle one!"

"Ouch! Taste my boot!"

"I have. It has a flavour of worldly attachment."

"You pompous buffoon!"

"Argh! Ugh! Eek!"

¶ This is based on a true story. I really did meet a Buddhist who liked to brag about how much he had reduced his ego that week.

60 THE IMPROBABLE VELOCIPEDE

A rich and powerful madman clapped his hands and said, "See that tall mountain over there? I want you to remove it from its base and set it on two wheels; then I want you to connect the back wheel to a system of gears and pedals, so that a climber sitting on the summit of the peak can make the whole thing trundle along."

"That's a really big job," people warned him.

"So what? I'm rich and powerful and I can easily afford it. Do what I say with minimal delay!"

Six months later it was ready. As the madman pedalled the mass of rock and ice along, sounding his alpenhorn at pedestrians, he chuckled to himself. "I've always wanted a mountain bike."

¶ And now he has got one.

61 A TOWN NAMED DÉJÀ

There was a town named Déjà and it was a small place without much in the way of sights. Two tourists went there on vacation anyway. One of the tourists was a giant gastropod; the other was an old steam-powered robot. They were just good friends.

After visiting the museum and its collection of gnomes, and spending time in the local restaurants, they were bored. There was nothing else to do. "Although this is the first time I've been here, I don't ever want to come back," yawned the gastropod.

An aardvark overheard them. "I'm on vacation too and I'm having a great time. Why not explore the scenery around the town? There's a tall mountain that is easy to climb and the view from the top is excellent. I can't recommend it *highly* enough…"

The gastropod laughed at the pun but the robot said, "Why have you got apricot jam stains on your nose?"

"That's a long story," answered the aardvark.

"Bet it's not as long as your nose!" chortled the gastropod.

"Very droll," sighed the aardvark.

The gastropod and the robot walked out of town and headed towards the mountain. It took most of the day to climb to the top, but it was worth it. They stood on a ledge and looked down at the tiny town. A sign near them declared: DÉJÀ VIEW. The robot pondered for a few minutes and then said, "I think I've been here before."

"So have I," replied the gastropod. "So have I."

¶ This moral seems familiar. This moral seems familiar.

62 THE SEA SERPENT AND THE ROWING BOAT

A sea serpent fell in love with a rowing boat. "I love you. Do you love me in return?" asked the sea serpent.

"Yes, I think so," replied the rowing boat.

"Despite the enormous age difference? I mean, I'm a living fossil from the Jurassic period but you were constructed in 1959; and the trees from which you are made aren't older than a hundred years. Are you sure you wouldn't prefer a younger monster?"

The rowing boat dismissed her anxieties.

"Don't be silly," he said. "It's my *design* that matters, not my building materials. And that dates back several thousand years at least. So put your mind at rest and let's get smoochy!"

The sea serpent was happy to be formally courted by the rowing boat. Every day he brought her a little gift, usually a human being that she was able to devour in one tasty gulp.

One afternoon the rowing boat turned up with a man dressed in a frock coat and top hat. This man struggled with the oars but he wasn't in control and had to go where the rowing boat wanted. Then the rowing boat cried out, "Look honey! A saint for you!"

The sea serpent surfaced at that point. "A saint?"

"I thought it was time we got properly engaged. That is how much I love you! It occurred to me that a saint's halo could be used as a ring. It's up to you whether you accept or not…"

The sea serpent examined the occupant of the boat.

"It's a very sweet idea," she said, "and of course I would accept. But I don't think this fellow is a saint. He looks more like an industrialist. And he doesn't have a halo, just a top hat."

"He's in disguise. His halo is *beneath* the hat!"

"So it is! How odd! Yum!"

¶ Keep it under your hat by all means, but that won't save you.

63 THE APPRENTICE

A bag of sugar wanted to hire an apprentice. In fact he wanted a business partner that would have the ideas and do all the work, while he, the bag of sugar, provided cash, contacts and clout.

A loaded blunderbuss arrived to be interviewed.

The bag of sugar said, "When I was your age, all I had was a thousand pounds and the support of my parents, plus another forty thousand in the bank, a car and two mobile phones. I couldn't speak Japanese, Russian or Martian, but I still made it *on my own*."

"Well done," replied the blunderbuss.

"Let's see your business plan," growled the bag of sugar.

The blunderbuss was nervous. "If you point me and pull the trigger I'm guaranteed to hit my target every time."

"Really?" scoffed the bag of sugar. "That sounds a little bit 'corporate' to me. I want a demonstration right now!"

There was a loud detonation and a cloud of smoke.

The bag of sugar was annoyed.

"You're fired!" he growled to the blunderbuss.

"How very observant of you," came the calm reply, "but you forgot to mention that the ricochet has perforated you and all your sugar is trickling away and soon there will be none left."

¶ Big shots are often felled by little shots.

64 THE ITCHY PLANET

Venus said to the planet Mars, "What's the weather like in your region of space? I'm sweltering over here!"

"Rather chilly, as a matter of fact," replied Mars.

"That's a shame," said Venus.

"Are you just making small talk or do you have something important to say to me?" asked Mars directly.

Venus blushed and said, "Well, I couldn't help noticing that you have a couple of fleas on you. I wasn't sure if you were aware of them or not. It's a delicate subject to discuss."

Mars sighed deeply. "Some of the insects that infest planet Earth have managed to launch a space expedition to me. The spot where they landed is very itchy now and I think they are taking geological samples. I would love to scratch but I daren't do so."

"Why? Will scratching make it worse?"

"Maybe but that's not my reason for not scratching. My reason is that I don't have any arms. I'm a planet, you see."

"So am I," observed Venus.

"Yes, but your conditions are too inhospitable to attract their attention. Maybe I can ask a comet to smash into their spacecraft and annihilate it, trapping the astronauts on my surface until they run out of air. That might possibly discourage future expeditions."

"Do you know any comets?" Venus asked.

"Only Bill Haley," said Mars.

"I'm sure he will agree to help," replied Venus, "and if he can't do it personally, maybe he'll send a meteorite instead. I seem to recall that he runs a 24 hour meteorite service called 'Rock Around the Clock' but that might well be an honest mistake."

"Not honest," said Mars, "just contrived…"

¶ Psst! Venus and Mars are having an affair. Don't spread it about.

65 COLD TEDDY

A teddy bear was thrown into the sea. It drifted north until it reached the Arctic Ocean. Then the waters froze and it found itself trapped on pack ice near the island of Spitsbergen.

59

There are such things as Polar Bears, of course, but the teddy wasn't one of those, so it didn't feel comfortable in this environment. Indeed, it was so upset and lonely that it began to cry and one by one the big tears landed on the ice and froze rapidly.

These tears made a shape as they accumulated.

"A wolf! It's a wolf!" cried the teddy.

A passing walrus said, "Why should I be scared of that? For one thing, I don't believe you. You are a liar."

The teddy was shocked. "Why do you say that?"

"Because you're the toy that cried wolf," said the walrus.

The teddy scratched its head. "But doesn't that generate a paradox? If you don't believe that I made a wolf with my frozen tears because I'm the toy that cried wolf, then you don't believe what you've already decided to accept as the truth. You're using the fact that something exists to disprove that same something. That's a bit odd."

But the walrus reacted with rage to this observation.

"Don't ruin my pun, you meanie!"

¶ To ruin the pun of a walrus is no easy tusk, I mean task.

66 THE HOT GEYSEROO

A hot geyseroo was hopping along when a cryptozoologist happened to notice it and shout, "What are you?"

"I'm a geyseroo, the hot kind," came the reply.

The cryptozoologist leafed through his bestiary and checked the index but he couldn't find any reference to that monster in the book. "You must be extremely rare," he remarked.

"Yes, that's true," concurred the hot geyseroo.

"What's that in your pouch?"

"It's a baby xaratan. That's what hot geyseroos do. They keep xaratans in their pouches until they are old enough to be set adrift on the ocean and pretend to be islands. It's our duty."

"Do you get paid for doing that?" asked the cryptozoologist.

"Nah, it's purely voluntary."

"But why can't I discern your outline or form a picture of your body in my mind when I close my eyes?"

The hot geyseroo said, "Because the fellow who wrote this fable didn't bother to describe me, that's why."

"I see. He just left you deliberately vague?"

"Yep. Well, I must be off."

"Nice to meet you. Take care. Bye!"

As the hot geyseroo bounded away, the xaratan in its pouch looked up and said, "What the heck was that?"

"A cryptozoologist," answered the hot geyseroo.

The xaratan rustled some pages.

"I can't find one of those listed in my reference book of humans. Are they especially rare, I wonder? I can't even form a coherent picture of his body in my mind when I close my eyes."

"Don't bother. He was ugly," said the hot geyseroo.

¶ Make up your own moral for this fable.

67 PLAYGROUND FIGHT

A class of antibodies was waiting anxiously for the bell that signalled the lunchtime break. It was a very boring lesson; a dose of sugar was talking about how to succeed in business.

At last the bell rang and the antibodies rushed out.

"Don't forget to do your homework!" cried the annoyed dose of sugar after them. And then he muttered quietly to himself, "If I was a bag rather than just a dose of sugar, and if I owned a large company, I'd make sure that all those little brats were fired!"

Out on the playground the antibodies played with conkers, marbles and footballs. Suddenly there was an invasion of hostile germs from a rival school. "Scrap!" yelled the germs.

"Scrap! Scrap!" echoed the antibodies.

"We're going to bash you!"

"You and whose army? Come and get it!"

"Pow! Ugh! Suppurate!"

The dose of sugar glanced out of the window and sighed. "This is the last time I teach inside a bloodstream."

He went to complain to the headmaster, who shrugged. "Antibodies and germs will always fight each other. There's nothing you can do. It's just biology. Bodies will be bodies."

Then the headmaster laughed and so did the sugar.

¶ The headmaster's laughter was infectious.

68 THE LOST FABLE

A fable that was lost burst into tears. "I don't belong in this collection of postmodern fripperies. I'm a decent fable, not a facile whimsy, and I was originally part of a traditional collection with real morals and everything. This Rhysop fellow has debased the form with his travesties and I want no part of his despicable project."

A passing crow asked, "What's the issue?"

The fable told him and the crow replied that he knew a clever earwig who could easily solve his problem.

So the fable set off on a long journey and eventually reached the cave where the earwig lived. When the earwig asked him what the matter was, the fable said, "Can you take me out of this set of facile fables and put me into Aesop's collection instead?"

"Are you sure about that?" the earwig asked.

The fable nodded, so the earwig went to consult one of his books of magic and then he waved his legs in a special way and the fable vanished from sight. "What a strange request!" muttered the earwig to himself, as he went back to playing scales on the zither; he was learning the zither in his spare time. Why the devil not?

The fable opened its eyes and found itself wedged among dozens of used napkins and handkerchiefs. "This isn't the middle of Aesop's Fables! Where are the hare and the tortoise and all the other favourites? All I can see are snot rags and stained bibs!"

Across time and space floated the voice of the earwig. "The historical Aesop was a slave. He didn't actually write down his fables. And he didn't have enough money or opportunity to indulge any normal hobbies, so he made do with collecting bits of discarded cloth. This is the only *collection* Aesop ever had in his lifetime..."

"Now he bloody tells me!" groaned the fable.

¶ Nobody knows for certain if Aesop was even a real person.

69 CLOUDCUCKOOLAND

A tectonic plate laid a clutch of continents. To keep them safe, it made a nest of fluffy cumulus clouds in the sky and put the unhatched continents inside. But while it was absent, another tectonic plate came along and laid a continent of its own among them.

The first tectonic plate soon returned but it didn't realise anything was amiss and it sat on the new addition without suspecting it wasn't a rightful landmass. Time passed. The false continent was the first to hatch and then it instinctively pushed out the others.

"Feed me! Feed me!" it shrieked blindly.

The foster mother was kept busy collecting the trappings of advanced civilisations to satisfy it and "I'm worn out," it gasped one day. "You are more demanding than I anticipated."

The cuckoo continent considered this and said:

"Don't worry. It's time for me to leave the nest anyway. Thanks for all the temples, coffee shops and monorails you adorned me with! I think I'll settle down in the Gulf of Mexico."

"Shame about your brothers and sisters," said the tectonic plate. "I still find it strange how you accidentally nudged them out of the nest like that. Poor little Atlantis, Lemuria and Mu!"

"Yes, I guess they are lost continents now."

¶ Don't leave unhatched continents unattended.

70 VERNE YOUR KEEP

"Look here," said the professor as he picked up the parchment that had fallen out of the dusty antique book. "It's an ancient map that shows how an explorer can reach the centre of—"

"Do we have to go there?" gasped his nephew.

"Yes Axel," nodded the professor.

"My name's not Axel," objected the nephew.

"Isn't it?" cried the professor.

"No, I'm afraid it's not," said Hubcap.

"Well, that doesn't really matter, dear boy. The crucial thing is that we set off on an expedition immediately. Pack your things now. Then I'll hire a guide called Hans, if I can find one."

A few hours later the intrepid pair were ready. By carefully following the directions of the mysterious map, they caught a bus and reached their destination without getting lost. They didn't have a guide called Hans but a pickle jar named Roger turned out to be good enough. They got off the bus and wandered around the shops.

"My name isn't Roger," said the pickle jar.

When they had spent most of their money they decided to return home but they thought it would be fun to emerge from the crater of a volcano. They looked everywhere for one, and even asked various pedestrians, but it seemed there was a general shortage of such geographical features in the region. So they caught the bus back.

The professor said, "Tomorrow morning I'll start writing my account of the voyage. I won't give it a fancy title; I'll just call it *Journey to the Centre of Perth*. If it's successful maybe we can use the royalties to fund other expeditions to Australian cities?"

¶ Boris the pickle jar got smashed later.

71 THE SCARED GHOST

There was a ghost who was scared of life. "But you're already dead and the danger is over," pointed out a skeleton.

"D-d-d-don't tempt fate!" shivered the ghost.

"What is it exactly about life that alarms you so much?" the skeleton asked. The ghost turned *elap* and began...

"One moment!" cried the skeleton. "What is 'elap'?"

"The opposite of pale," answered the ghost. "Living men and women turn pale when they are scared; so it follows that a frightened ghost will turn elap. That's logical, isn't it?"

The skeleton waved a bony hand. "Fair enough. Continue."

"I've forgotten what I was going to say..."

"It can't have been important, in that case," said the skeleton.

The ghost shrugged. "Maybe not."

"What are you doing tonight?" asked the skeleton.

"Are you hitting on me?"

"Yes, I am. I've fancied you for ages."

"As it happens, I'm free. What did you have in mind?"

"How about the cinema?"

"I don't know. What are they showing?"

"A romance. It's all about a man and a woman who meet on a train and fall in love and kiss each other with lips. Then they get married and dwell happily ever after in a nice house."

The ghost recoiled. "No! I hate horror films!"

¶ One dead thing's date is another dead thing's nightmare.

72 ABUNDANCE OF ROOTS

There was a tree with lots of roots that showed above ground. Some of the other trees in the forest thought it was trying to be a showoff and they kept castigating it. "Tuck your roots in!"

"I can't," replied the tree. "I'm a tree and therefore can't move a muscle and in fact I don't *have* any muscles..."

"That's no excuse! What if someone trips over them?"

And in fact lots of animals did.

Not just animals. Other things that came along too.

A pig, a waffle, a box, a chump, a resentment, a caterpillar, a gift, a loom, a cuttlefish, an aurora borealis, a duvet, a chair, a sunken continent, a cup that runneth over, an ancient paradox, a snivel, a bone, a toothless cog, a piecrust, a passionate kiss, an aching thigh, a broken window, a phantom, a cat, a bathtub, a chimney clogged with twigs, a forced laugh, a chewed pencil, a beetroot stain, a vague feeling, a hovercraft, an argument, a dog, an example of jargon, a butterfly, a solecism and even a grotesque fiend and a coconut shy...

They all tripped over different roots. Sixty-five things in total tripped over sixty-five exposed roots. Imagine!

One day a confident papaya happened along; it tripped over the next root in the sequence. But it didn't just pick itself up and continue on its way. It kicked the root in question and kept kicking it. Not just a dozen kicks, not even a score, but hundreds!

¶ Get your kicks on root sixty-six.

73 SEEKER AFTER WISDOM

A beautiful seeker after profound wisdom was sitting in the lotus position in the park with a serene smile and a thick book of wise sayings open on her lap. This book consisted of aphorisms and snippets of advice from the greatest philosophers and religious leaders in the history of the world and it emphasised tolerance, patience, peace, compassion and tranquillity plus sincere respect for all living creatures.

Suddenly a wasp flew towards her face. Emitting a painful shriek, the seeker after wisdom slammed the book shut, crushing the insect flat and ending its life.

After a few deep breaths, she resumed reading. "Om!" she chanted as her delicate soul normalised.

¶ We are all hypocrites: you, me and the next-door neighbour.

74 THE EMERGENCY AARDVARK

An aeroplane was preparing to take off.

"If anything bad happens, such as engine failure or a collision with a sentient hot-air balloon," said a flight attendant to the passengers, "then you must remember not to panic. This aircraft is fitted with an emergency aardvark and he'll sort everything out."

The aeroplane lifted into the sky. But it flew directly into a storm and blue lightning bolts broke off the wings. Before the passengers could start screaming, the emergency aardvark appeared among them. "Hey, why do you have apricot jam smeared along your nose?" someone demanded of him.

"It's a long story," replied the aardvark. "Now what appears to be the trouble? Can anybody please tell me?"

"The wings have broken off! Can you replace them?"

"Um, not really. I only do termites."

The passengers were annoyed and shook their fists before they hit the ground and were mangled to horrid bits.

"Bloody airline! We're not flying *Aardvarkflot* again!"

¶ No aardvark is an engineer.

75 THE MARTIAN CORACLES

Millennia ago, when the surface of the planet Mars was covered in water, the denizens of that planet sailed along the canals in little round boats. It was a curious fact that these inhabitants could be divided into three races based on their inherent characteristics.

The first race liked to hang around places, usually while carrying their coracles on their backs. They always tried to avoid being seen. Often they snickered and rubbed their hands together.

The second race told many jokes; they were always joking, even when it wasn't appropriate for them to do so. They joked whether they were in or out of their coracles, at all times of day.

The third race was very religious and they preferred to communicate with the deities they believed in. They did this by paddling their coracles to various sacred spots around the planet, closing their eyes and muttering words to the gods or goddesses in question.

¶ A Mars a day helps you lurk, jest and pray.

76 MIGHT BE TRIPLE

Gerald liked dressing up in a suit of armour. One day he met a friend who said to him, "I'm holding a fancy dress party on Thursday night. I want to take this opportunity to invite you."

"Thanks, but I can't make it. I've got something on."

"Have you? What's that then?"

"A suit of armour, of course!" cried Gerald.

There was an awkward pause...

The friend leaned forward and peered at Gerald's chest. "Do you spend a lot of time polishing your breastplate? I can see a reflection in it, but it's not my face. It looks like Confucius!"

"That," said Gerald, "is the chink in my armour."

But the friend was outraged.

"Anyone who stoops to making a racist remark for the sake of a joke is beneath contempt!" he growled.

Gerald sighed. "True, but you are also an integral part of this fable and thus equally responsible for the crassness of my remark. In fact, you're a worse offender than me because you resorted to a technique that Umberto Eco called *ironic double coding*."

"Will you kindly explain what that is?"

"It means communicating or propagating an idea while simultaneously pre-empting criticism for it. Had you been genuinely offended by my joke you would have refused to appear in this fable right at the beginning, for without your presence I wouldn't have had anyone to make my comment to. But by allowing the fable to proceed and then claiming to be offended later, you have merely sanitised it and thus helped yourself and the author to avoid blame. That's despicable."

¶ Is this an example of ironic triple coding? I don't know.

77 BANANA DRAMA

In an old monastery deep in the mountains in a fair country, a community of religious men grew their own food, and because the climate was warm, unlike that of Wales, they were able to harvest bananas and other tropical fruit. But the monks' regime was very strict and they were obliged to lock themselves in their cells every evening at sunset. One of the monks was a pervert and late one evening he lost his key and couldn't lock his door. He went searching for it on tiptoes and explored all the deserted passages and halls but he couldn't find it anywhere.

The following morning the community was mortified to learn that the bananas on all the trees had been eaten.

"This is the work of a monk key!" cried the abbot, "and it must belong to someone here. I will find out who!"

The pervert decided he might as well confess his guilt.

"Yes, it was entirely my fault," he said. "I liked to spank my monk key and it escaped last night and obviously went on an eating rampage. But in my defence, the pun doesn't really work. If you try too hard to force a pun it'll simply go on strike, like a miner."

"You're right about that. You're absolved," said the abbot.

¶ Puns only work for themselves.

78 GHOST IN THE MACHINE

A ghost once used its entire deathtime's savings to purchase a mainframe computer, to make possible the calculation of some of the parameters of the afterlife, I don't know which ones. But after operating for many hours at a frantic pace, the device froze.

"Bother!" exclaimed the ghost. "It must be jammed on the inside. I had better find out what the trouble is."

The ghost was the romantic partner of a skeleton and didn't want to be the victim of sarcasm when it became obvious what a waste of money the machine had been. "I ought to try and fix it before 'Bones' gets back," the ghost said to itself in desperation.

So it floated through the computer and ended up on the inside, but one of its wisps got snagged on a diode and it couldn't get back out. When the skeleton returned from work and heard the cries for help emanating from within the mainframe, it was astonished and thought there was some deep symbolic meaning in this incident.

"I didn't know computers had souls!" it gasped.

¶ They don't yet; but one day they might.

79 THE EARWIG'S WISH

Visitors kept interrupting an earwig that was learning to play the zither. They had heard he was clever and skilled in the arts of magic and could make their wishes come true, so they went on long journeys to speak to him and engage his services. After several years of this he still couldn't play any jazz on his chosen instrument.

One of the reasons more and more people set off to find him was that a crow spread the news to everyone he met.

"I wish I'd never told that crow about my powers," the earwig sighed to himself, "because he keeps advertising my existence and all sorts of odd beings turn up here at my cave. I can't get any peace at all. It's quite rubbish, truly it is, and I'm fed up!"

Then he stopped and thought. "Wait a moment... If that's what I wish, then why don't I make it come true?"

He went to consult his books of magic and soon had the right spell, so he waved his legs in a special way. There was a puff of smoke. And far away, a crow passed over a fox and a carrot that were loitering in a field and said, "What are you arguing about?"

"Salads," came the answer.

"Well," said the crow, "there's a solution to your problem. I know of a clever ear— Um, wait a moment! I've forgotten what I was going to say to you. In fact I don't think I knew in the first place!"

"Do you wish you had a better memory?" asked the fox and carrot.

"Yes, I suppose I do," said the crow.

"In that case," they continued, "allow us to recommend a magic square that might be able to help you. She's a square but she's also a circle, don't ask us how, and she lives in a cave not far from here..."

¶ In situations where insects can't help, geometry sometimes can.

74

80 THE MOTHERLODE

A gold miner went into a tunnel with a pick and shovels and hacked at the rock face with great enthusiasm. He knew that a rich seam of the precious yellow metal could be found deep inside the mountain that towered over his head. He kept in touch with a colleague outside by calling back along the tunnel. All day he worked hard.

Half an hour before sunset, an excited shout came out of the tunnel's mouth. "I've hit the motherlode!"

"Good for you!" his colleague answered.

There was a long pause and then howls. The terrified gold miner came running at top speed out of the tunnel.

"Flee for your life!" he advised his colleague.

"What's the matter?" puffed his colleague as they raced away from the scene. "I thought our luck had changed at last. You informed me that you had hit the motherlode, didn't you?"

The gold miner nodded. "Yes I did. But the fatherlode came back from work early and saw me hitting his wife. He wasn't very happy about that, I can tell you! He's a mean mother."

¶ The fatherlode is a mother? I'm confused!

81 SETTING OFF AGAIN

A knife and a book that had tried to steal and ride a bicycle but had failed to control the machine decided to hire a rickshaw instead. They stood on the street and hailed a passing vehicle.

"Are you a rickshaw?" they asked hopefully.

"Rick Shaw? He's my cousin. Hop in and I'll take you to him!"

The knife and book jumped inside.

"Is it far to go?" they asked.

"Yes it is," answered the driver, "for he lives in the capital of the robot world, which is a city made of transparent building materials. When I said he was my 'cousin' I wasn't being strictly accurate. He's a robot, just like I am. But don't hold that against him."

"How long will it take?" the knife and book persisted.

"About ten minutes in this thing."

"But why do robots even need a capital city?"

"It's quite simple. When a—"

"Look out!" screeched the knife and book. "You almost collided with that fox and carrot! Stop talking over your shoulder. Keep your eyes on the road, your hands upon the wheel."

"What do you mean? There is no road. This is an air-car!"

¶ Rick Shaw's wife is named Anne Droid.

82 THE CONDENSATION REPUBLIC

The drifting cold steam made a speech. It said, "Last week, I voted myself prime minister of the Condensation Republic. I am now in the process of dismantling the constitution and declaring myself a dictator, with ultimate control over the freezing and evaporation of all relevant droplets. The days of democratic condensation are over! Soon my clammy rule will extend into every bathroom on the planet! Some of those who have wiped their mirrors since my coup say that my victories over the forces of liberal condensation show me in a more virulent, less forgiving mood. Whatever the humidity, I intend to drip on several levels: wood, glass, bronze, leather and plastic."

The door was broken down. The armed mob entered the room.

"Surrender, your reign is over!"

"Already? But I've hardly done any dictating yet…"

"And we're here to stop you."

"What a bunch of spoilsports. Why do you all have so many arms? That chap over there, for instance, has at least a hundred of them, with two hands on the end of each."

"We came well armed in case you tried to pull our legs."

¶ Please enquire regarding overseas vapours.

83 FEELING BLUE

A parrot said to itself, "I'm blue, so why don't I form a blues band?" And it flew off to recruit some members. It found a blue sheep willing to play the drums, a blue goat that could pluck a bass and a blue giraffe to strum chords on a battered five-string guitar. The parrot gave itself the task of singing bluesy words to the music.

When the band was ready they played their first gig in a small bar but were booed off stage. "You aren't good enough! Come back a year from now, but be sure to sell your souls first in exchange for some ability. The Devil is happy to make the bargain."

"Well, I don't intend doing *that*," said the parrot.

Neither did any of the others...

"We need some advice on how to play better," the parrot decided. So they set off to visit a wise sage who knew the secrets of happiness. It had occurred to the parrot that if someone who knows all about happiness is turned upside-down he should know about sadness too, because sadness is the other side of happiness; and blues music is made of sadness, in the same way that skeletons are made of bones.

When they finally encountered the sage, they turned him upside-down and asked him for the secret of how to play the blues properly. The sage replied instantly, "Take it to the bridge."

This was curious advice, but the parrot and the other animals didn't dare argue, so they set off again and looked for a blue bridge. Finally they found one and recruited it into the band. But whether they become more successful as a result, I just don't know.

¶ Always invert a sage if you get the chance.

84 THE LUCKY BLACK CAT

A black cat said to itself, "Why don't I build a time machine so I can go back into the past and cross my own path?"

It constructed a time machine from old cat food tins and travelled back a few weeks; then it lay in wait for itself. As soon as it saw itself coming, it jumped out and crossed its own path.

"Hey, what are you doing?" it demanded of itself.

"Crossing your path to give you paradoxical but powerful good luck. I am from your future and want you to be lucky. This isn't altruism but an example of enlightened self-interest."

"But if you are me in the future, then you must already know whether the good luck worked or not! Did it?"

The black cat nodded. "Oh yes! I became so lucky that I was able to construct a time machine from inappropriate components even though I never studied physics at university."

The black cat digested this information and frowned. "What *did* you study there?" he asked suspiciously.

"Same as you," said the black cat. "Modern History."

¶ Felines are generally more accomplished in the humanities than the sciences, but you do get the odd maverick.

85 DIPLOMATIC IMMUNITY

An antibody met a germ and said, "How do you do? I am very happy to make your acquaintance. Would you like a cup of tea? May I fetch you a small cake? If you require anything to improve your comfort, please let me know and I'll do my best to provide it. I like your colour, shape and other physical characteristics. You are cool. You are grand. What a fine germ you are! I admire you so much."

"Well, that reaction wasn't what I was expecting!" cried the germ. "I came here to infect this bloodstream, but I don't think I'll do that now. I am too charmed by your kind words."

"It's a new style of resistance and I'm glad it seems to work. It's called diplomatic immunity," said the antibody.

¶ Germs that overstay their welcome are worse than relatives.

86 THE WALNUT WHIP

"I really fancy a walnut whip," said a man to his wife one evening. So she opened a cupboard door, took one out and started lashing him with it. The man cowered beneath the blows. "What are you doing?" he wailed, as his clothes were torn to shreds. "Stop it!"

"I'm giving you what you asked for," said his wife.

"That's more of a cat o' nine nuts than a normal walnut whip!" gasped the man, "but I suppose you're right."

¶ Some wives are always right and it can be painful.

87 IN A FLAP

"Look at me!" cried the flying machine that flapped its wings and had no propeller. "I'm looping the loop!"

"Yes, very good," sighed the glider.

"I love you. Here's a box of chocolates as a gift."

"Thanks. Very thoughtful."

"And some flowers…"

"Brilliant."

"Shall we go for a moonlit flight later?"

"Oh come on!" groaned the glider. "What are you? An ornithopter or a cornythopter?"

¶ When you spread your wings, keep your clichés to yourself.

88 SKELETON OF CONTENTION

A bone of contention got together with some other bones of contention and made a skeleton. It is quite draughty being a skeleton, so it slapped dough onto itself and went out in the hot sun, which baked the dough into bread muscles. Then it clothed itself in a pair of linen trousers and a linen shirt and strolled off along the beach.

But the smell of freshly baked bread attracted the seagulls that dived and pecked at the skeleton's exposed false flesh until only a few scraps remained on its skull, hands and feet.

"Now I look even sillier than before!" it huffed.

A beach bum was sprawled on a dune. "Hey buddy," he called to the skeleton, "Can you spare any dough?"

"Piss off!" bellowed the skeleton of contention.

¶ Crumbs!

89 TURNING THE OTHER CHEEK

A monkey that had more than two cheeks on its face was sprawled on the ground when a clever sage who knew everything there is to know about religion, philosophy and ethics happened to pass by. "Why do you look so sad and angry?" the sage enquired.

"I imagine it's because I keep getting insulted," said the monkey, "on account of my utterly freakish visage."

"And that's why you are lying in the dirt, is it?"

"Yes, I'm prone with hairy despair."

The sage snorted and answered, "Whenever someone hurts you, turn the other cheek. That's all you need to do. Try it and you'll go far, believe me. I'm a sage and full of wisdom."

The monkey considered his advice.

"Fair enough, I will," he said.

And because he needed the practice, he started turning the other cheek immediately; but because he had so many of them, and because they went right around his head, he began rolling along the ground. He went faster and faster as he kept turning them, accelerating like a horizontal tornado that stank of banana juice and peanuts.

Soon he had vanished over the horizon. The sage smiled.

"I said he'd go far, didn't I?"

¶ A cheeky monkey gathers no moss.

90 THE ASTRAL DOGGERS

An astronaut was about to enter the capsule of his spaceship when a man rushed up with an autograph book. "I'm a big fan of interplanetary heroes. Will you please sign your name for me?"

The astronaut obliged. "Certainly. Here you are."

But the fan grew even more excited. "It must be superb to be launched in a rocket and see the amazing sights of the universe. What wonders did you observe the last time you took off?"

The astronaut answered, "I saw you having vigorous sex with a buxom freckled redhead in a clearing in the woods."

"Really?" cried the autograph hunter, much embarrassed.

"Of course. Why else do you think we travel so far and put telescopes into orbit? It isn't to gaze at boring stars!"

"You mean to say that the whole point of the space program is to spy on frisky couples having sex outdoors?"

The astronaut nodded. "From a space station or from the surface of the moon, we can see nearly everything that happens. People just assume we are looking outwards into deep space. In fact our eyes and instruments are trained downwards on people like you."

"But what would happen if you were caught peeping?"

"I'd say I was walking the dog."

"Surely that's impossible!" objected the fan.

The astronaut shook his head and laughed. "Don't you know anything about the history of space flight? Why do you think a dog was sent up before humans? Yes, it's true. A dog called Laika was launched into orbit aboard Sputnik 2 in 1957. There's a clue in the name 'Sputnik', don't you think? We're all voyeurs. Woof woof."

¶ This is Ground Control to Major Peeping Tom.

91 THE WEATHER STATION

A skint skunk, an old steam-powered robot, an odd-job man called Tim, a hot geyseroo and an elephant that was fond of practical jokes were fed up with the fact that the weather was always bad. "Let's march to the nearest weather station and lodge a complaint!"

And that's what they did. They barged down the door of the building and rushed into the main room where all the forecasting took place. But instead of a bank of computers connected to meteorological equipment, they found a man on his knees rolling dice.

"So that's how they do forecasts!" bellowed the robot.

"It stinks, I tell you!" growled the skunk.

"I'm going to write a letter of complaint!" said the geyseroo.

"This is far too fishy," cried Tim.

But the elephant was less impulsive. It thought for a moment and then said gently, "Wait a moment! Of course the weather is always going to be bad. This man is playing craps!"

¶ In Wales the weather is always crap anyway.

92 AN EPIC REALISATION

The characters in *The Iliad* turned to the characters in *The Odyssey* and said, "We've just realised something!"

"Tell us and be quick about it. The cyclops is coming!"

"All the lovers in our story, and all the lovers in your story, even the straight ones, are Homer-sexuals."

"Too late, we are being devoured. Argh!"

¶ When is Homer going to write the third part of that trilogy? I've been waiting for ages.

93 THE TRAINING COACH

An amateur athlete who wanted to boost his performance decided to hire a professional coach. The arrangements were made by telephone. The coach promised to meet the athlete on the beach the following morning at sunrise.

When the athlete turned up, the sun hadn't yet risen; so he did a few light exercises to warm up. Suddenly there was the roar of an old engine and a horrible bus came over a dune.

"Stop! Stop!" cried the athlete, but there was no driver.

The bus ran him over and then applied its brakes.

"I wonder where the athlete is? I was supposed to meet him here at sunrise. Maybe I'm a little early," said the coach to itself. Then it blinked its headlights and yawned its radiator grille.

¶ Better a training coach than a coaching train. Choo choo!

94 GOOSE WRITING ADVICE

"Hey, what are you doing?" cried a goose as it waddled past a man who was brushing tar all over the manuscript of an unpublished book. "Why are you coating that tome with the sticky thick residue of the petroleum industry? That is peculiar behaviour!"

"I'm pitching my new novel," came the answer.

"You fool!" cackled the goose. "You're supposed to proofread it, not waterproof it. But the real issue is that you're supposed to pitch the idea to a publisher first, not the actual book."

"Pitch the idea?" frowned the man.

"That's the way it is usually done," confirmed the goose.

"But the idea is contained in the manuscript, embodied by the prose I have employed to tell the story that occurs, so by pitching the book I am also pitching the idea within, aren't I?"

"You employed prose? What wages did you pay it?"

"Don't try to be hilarious, bird!"

The goose said, "Well, pitching a novel is no use if the idea is smeared over and thus can't be appreciated."

The man considered this. "I see your point. Luckily the idea still exists in my head. I keep a copy there. So if I pitch my head, but leave a gap so the idea can still be viewed from outside, I'll stand a better chance of my novel being published. Is that right?"

"Yes. It works for me," replied the goose.

So the man began coating his head with tar and eventually only one of his ears jutted out from the black mess.

¶ What's right for a goose is wrong for a writer.

95 THE GLOVE

"I wish I could fly!" sighed a glove. "It's true that I enjoy surfing waves; but waves only occur when the person who waves me lifts their hand and makes a gesture meaning hello or goodbye. Flying is surely superior to surfing or any other activity. I wish I knew the secret of rising into the air and staying there."

"I'll teach you to fly," offered a sentient hot-air balloon who happened to be drifting past. And he did exactly that. He showed the glove how to fill itself with hydrogen gas and seal itself at the wrist. Away flew the glove and thanks to a bizarre meteorological phenomenon involving the lower atmosphere acting like a magnifying lens, the flying item of handy fashion appeared much bigger than it really was, dominating the whole sky.

¶ Glove is in the air: everywhere you look around.

96 EDUCATED SHAPES

A myopic triangle that had gone to university to study economics became friendly with a segment and one day said, "Will you come dancing with me tonight? Then maybe we could go for a walk in the moonlight. I like you very much, to be perfectly candid."

The segment blushed. "I must reject your amorous proposal for the simple reason that we're not compatible."

"What do you mean? We are both young triangles."

The segment shook its head. "I'm not. You must be very shortsighted indeed. One of my sides is curved. I'm a segment, part of a circle. In fact I came to university in the first place to graduate as a complete circle, but it's taking a very long time, I'm afraid."

"Pardon my mistake!" cried the mortified triangle.

"I have been at this university for a hundred years already," sighed the segment, "and I probably won't leave for another century or two. I have studied so many subjects I feel sick!"

"But why can't you graduate sooner than that?"

The segment answered sadly, "Because to become a proper accredited circle I require exactly 360 degrees."

¶ An uneducated circle only turns stomachs.

97 GREEN SOUP

A chef prepared a cauldron of green soup over a fire for his guests. He served it in deep bowls and most of the guests ate it with relish, but one fellow pulled a sour face. "Yuck!"

The chef was offended. "You don't like it?"

"What sort of green pea soup is this? From what pods did these peas come? They taste unmentionable!"

The chef raised an eyebrow. "Peas? I thought you wanted green pee soup. There has been a mistake…"

The man who had complained shuddered.

"How did you manage to get hold of green pee in sufficient quantities to fill your cauldron?" he enquired.

"I invited the patients of a local hospital to come round and take it in turns relieving themselves into the cooking pot," said the chef. "Most of them suffered from hideous and bizarre venereal diseases, which explains the particular colour of the liquid."

"It's true what they say," said the unhappy feaster, as he laid down his spoon. "Too many cocks spoil the broth!"

¶ Waiter! There's an undone fly in my soup!

98 UNDERMINING AUTHORITY

A mayor was about to make a long speech from a wooden platform that had been erected in a field. He planned to tell his audience how great he was and why they should vote for him again in the forthcoming elections. But a mole that lived under the ground had dug so many tunnels that the wooden stand collapsed and the mayor was cast down and bashed on the bonce and blood trickled from his head.

"That's the only free thing we'll get from him," said a raven among the spectators. "A minor flow of pale ichor."

"His ratings have certainly gone down," added a mouse.

"His popularity took a nosedive," said a fox, "and I doubt the nose in question will ever be straight again."

"At least he can see the issues from a grassroots level," added a rabbit with a triumphant twitch of its nose.

The mole surfaced with a groan. "If I'd known that you lot would seize any opportunity, however slight, to make puns, I wouldn't have bothered digging my tunnels in the first place."

¶ Moles obviously lack a sense of humour.

99 THE RABBIT IN THE BAKERY

A rabbit lived in a bakery and every morning he nibbled the buns so that he grew fatter and fatter and the profits were eaten into. The baker was so exasperated at this behaviour that he decided to confront the rabbit. "Why don't you eat grass or salad greens like other rabbits instead of the buns I bake? Your actions are ruining me!"

The rabbit blinked at the baker and twitched his ears.

The baker sighed and added, "I baked sixty currant buns last night and all of them have vanished. There are only a few crumbs left! Why did you devour them? There must be a reason."

"Yes, there is," agreed the rabbit. "I'm a *bunny*."

The baker didn't know what to say.

"Plus I'm pregnant again," explained the rabbit.

¶ Rabbits breed like hot cakes.

100 THE BUSTY WHORE

A busty whore allowed men to satisfy themselves in her cleavage and she never expected payment in cash. What she wanted in return was a few old clothes and two or three broken chairs.

One client, who happened to be a Viking who liked playing croquet with a gnome, questioned this idiosyncrasy. "Why do you allow the use of your bosom in return for such junk?"

"Well," replied the busty whore thoughtfully, "it's because I was told by my mother always to give tit for tat."

¶ You can lead a whore to culture but you can't make her think. Feel free to try, though. Just leave me out of it.

101 THE HIGHLY QUALIFIED NOSE

An aardvark went for a job interview. "Why do you have apricot jam on your nose?" was the first question.

"It's a long story," replied the aardvark.

"Not as long as your nose, I bet!" chuckled the horse who was conducting the interview. Probably he thought he was the first entity to make that joke.

"Look," said the aardvark reasonably. "I have all the qualities you require in a foreman of a spice factory. I can sniff and retrieve cardamom pods that have rolled under benches; I can sniff and retrieve chillies that have fallen behind jars; I can sniff and retrieve saffron that has—"

"Can you sniff and retrieve *this*?" cried the horse.

"Huh? Atchoo!!!"

The horse put away the sample of black pepper and pointed at the door with a hoof. "Sorry, I can't offer you the job. You have a highly qualified nose but when it came to the interview stage you blew it."

¶ The aardvark didn't really want that job anyway...

A face with measles was hoping to win first prize in the annual competition organised by the Polka Dot Society; it was just a huge face without a body or the rest of the head. But when the big night arrived, a ladybird turned out to have more appeal in the eyes of the judges.

The face went home and was very sad.

"Don't be too despondent," said the flintlock duelling pistol that lived in the same house. "You did your best and that's all anyone can ask. Seriously. All anyone can ask…"

"Is it really?" asked the face.

"Indeed," replied the pistol.

The face thought for a moment and then said, "What's the capital of Suriname? How far away is the star Polaris? Who was the ninth king of Atlantis?"

There was a long uncomfortable silence.

Then the pistol went off.

"I win!" it cried over the dying face.

¶ Anyone can always ask more. Be careful.

103 THE COSSACK

"What's the rush, huh?" a crane asked a passing Cossack.

"Rush, huh?" repeated the Cossack.

"That's what I said," said the crane.

"I'm not from Rush, huh," clarified the Cossack, "but from Ukraine. The difference is important."

"Ukraine?" came the reply. "Yes. Me crane, you Cossack. Isn't that obvious?"

¶ The most obvious things sometimes aren't.

104 A SMASHING EXCUSE

A genie lived happily in a green glass bottle until the bottle was accidentally smashed by a meteorite. The genie went on the rampage, getting drunk, taking drugs, starting fires in rubbish tips and stealing food from shops. "I hope you have a good excuse for your deplorable behaviour!" protested the meteorite.

The genie nodded. "Yes I do. I come from a broken home."

¶ The genies of today have no respect for the law.

105 CHAPPED LIPS

A beautiful girl was walking along a beach directly into a cold north wind. "My lips are chapped!" she moaned.

"No they're not. They are female lips," answered the north wind.

"That's incorrect," she told him. "I borrowed them from my boyfriend this morning in exchange for my hips."

¶ Less of your lip!

Paprika, coriander and cardamom were gossiping about the other spices in the cupboard. "We hate the way that nutmeg and fenugreek can't stop having sex with each other. It's disgusting."

A piece of ginger said, "I have just heard that the Spiceish Inquisition has banned loud sex under pain of torture."

"About time!" cried paprika. "That'll shut up nutmeg and fenugreek. I look forward to some peace and quiet."

"So do I," concurred coriander.

"Me too," said cardamom with a sigh.

"Hey you," called paprika to a jar that hadn't spoken yet. "Turmeric, is it? What's your opinion of all this?"

"I'm not turmeric, I'm cumin," was the reply.

"I beg your pardon? Speak up!"

"I'm cumin! I'm cumin! Oh, I'm cumin!"

The cupboard doors suddenly flew open and the agents of the Spiceish Inquisition reached inside and grabbed the culprit. "Having loud sex, are you? That's illegal! Come with us!"

"What will you do to him?" demanded ginger.

The agents turned and snarled, "Put him on the rack, of course — the spice rack! Now go back to work. Your job is to lose your flavour before you actually get used. Don't forget."

¶ Saffron the little spice jars to cumin unto me.

107 THE DRAGONFLY

A dragonfly skimmed along the water and its wings shimmered in the sun with many wonderful colours. "What a beautiful creature!" thought a cosmic explorer as he watched it.

He was visiting planet Earth from another dimension. "What a shame we don't have such beings in Jeopkaleoeoeo, the world where I come from. I wonder what it is called?"

A mouse that overhead the explorer said, "It's a dragonfly."

The explorer thanked the mouse. Much later, after he returned to his own dimension, he thought deeply about the significance of that name and he decided it was highly likely that it was a clue to the creature's biological composition. "I bet I can make my own dragonfly!" he said to himself. Then he set off on a journey.

He travelled to a dire region of gloomy caves and he soon encountered a dragon. "One moment!" he cried, as he dipped into a pocket for a jar. Inside the jar buzzed a fly he had caught earlier.

He tied the fly to the dragon with a piece of string.

Hey presto! A dragonfly!

"It doesn't look right," he muttered.

¶ The dragon toasted him a few seconds later.

108 TONGUEWAGGLE CHIPCHOP

The owner of a market stall went to see Tonguewaggle Chipchop, who was a lawyer. "I'm the guy in films," said the client, "who always owns a market stall that gets destroyed in a car chase."

"Ah yes, I've seen you in many action movies! How can I help?"

"I want to sue: not just for damages and loss of earnings but also for trauma (psychological). I want to sue the filmmakers so hard they'll never be able to afford another car chase."

Tonguewaggle arched his eyebrows. "I think I can win the case for you. I recently won a case on behalf of a badger named Bandit who sued a mammoth for destroying his bridge."

And the case went to court. And Mr Chipchop was so persuasive that the market stall owner won. The filmmakers were sued; they were left with so little money they couldn't afford a car.

But they made new films anyway.

And now all the chases are on bicycles or pogo sticks and the market stall still keeps getting destroyed.

¶ They don't make them like they used to.

109 MIDNIGHT IN THE MORNING

Night got drunk and lost all track of time. Soon after dawn he staggered into the day and brought the stars with him. It was very confusing for all the animals and plants; and even the clouds didn't know what to

97

do, how bright to shine, whether to let the moon peep through or not. The sun was intensely annoyed. "You utter moron!"

"Have I come the wrong way?" slurred Night.

"Yes, you bloody have. It's the morning. Look at the state of you! I can smell vacuum on your breath!"

"I tried to drink away my sorrows," said Night.

"Your sorrows!" sneered the sun. "What do *you* have to be sad about? You're not even a sentient creature. You're just a name for the period of darkness occasioned by my absence."

"My best friend, Twilight, has gone forever. She was offered a better job and I'll never see her again. She went to work for the Gods. She's the Twilight of the Gods now, not mine."

"I'm sure you'll get over it," sighed the sun.

"And Dusk, my other best friend, tripped over a loose paving slab and banged his head and died last night."

"Well, that *is* a shame," said the sun, "but it doesn't give you a reason to turn up in the sky at this hour."

"Yes it does! I'm in mourning. In mourning for Dusk!"

"Get a dictionary!" hissed the sun.

¶ There's a friendly living dictionary in Fable #51 he could use.

There was fable who knew he was part of a collection of fables, but he had no idea what number he was. "I could be anything! I could be the first or last or even the halfway point!"

He looked to right and left and saw other fables lurking there.

"On second thoughts, I can't be first or last; if that was the case I'd be on the end row and I would only have neighbours in one direction. I must be in the middle. How will I ever get to learn what number I am? I know! I'll ask the reader out there to tell me."

And that's exactly what he did. He asked you.

But you refused to tell him…

You smiled, grimaced, sighed or made a dozen other expressions, but not a single one of you opened your mouth to speak the answer aloud. Shame on you! Embarrassed to talk aloud to this page, are you? Worried in case anyone around you thinks you are mad for talking to yourself? I can't believe it. Poor little fable!

¶ I've got *your* number.

111 ACTING THE GOAT

A sheep decided to join the theatre. Her first role was to play a goat that got itself stuck at the top of a cliff.

The director told her that she had to convey fear, anguish and despair so convincingly that the people in the audience would believe the scripted predicament was real. But on the play's opening night, the woolly actress forgot her lines and began laughing.

The director was outraged and rushed onto the stage in full view of the audience. "Start acting the goat!" he cried.

¶ The audience were fleeced that night.

112 VAMPIRES!

A map hanging on the wall of a study said to a globe that was resting on a desk, "Repeat what you just told me."

"Australia is actually upside-down," said the globe.

"Are you sure?" cried the map.

"Yes," said the globe, checking his continents. "It's below my equator, in the Southern Hemisphere. Look!"

"So it is! So everything there is upside-down? The carrots, the foxes, the bicycles, gurus and gastropods?"

"Everything," agreed the globe.

The map was astonished. "And I guess this logically means that all the writing in all the books in Australia must also be inverted! In that case, I suppose the people of that strange country must stand on their heads each time they want to read something?"

"Or they might use mirrors," suggested the globe.

"Do they?" enquired the map.

"No, they don't. Australians never use mirrors when they read books. An Australian owned me once.

That's how I know. I saw her read two or three books but always without a mirror."

"I wonder why not? Mirrors must be dangerous to them for some odd reason. Or else they simply have no need of them in normal life. Perhaps mirrors don't work for them. But why?"

"If they don't have reflections, that would explain it."

"Yes, it would. But that means…"

The globe spun itself once on its own axis, which is equal to a shiver, and cried, "All Australians are vampires!"

¶ Mirrors reverse from side to side, not vertically. But Australians are probably vampires anyway. Runs in the blood.

113 ACTING THE GHOST

A goat decided to join the theatre. Her first role was to play a ghost that got itself stuck in a secret passage.

The director told her that she had to convey eeriness, melancholy and terror so convincingly that the people in the audience would believe the scripted predicament was real. But on the play's opening night, the goat forgot her lines and began laughing.

The director was outraged and rushed onto the stage in full view of the audience. "You ninny!" he roared.

"It's 'nanny', not 'ninny'," said the goat.

¶ How come ghosts always know about secret passages?

114 MORE VAMPIRES!

"Is it true," speculated the hatstand, "that a vampire has no reflection in a mirror?" He was nude at the moment, for no hats covered him. The table was also naked and was waiting to be laid.

"Yes," she said. "And in fact if you hang a large mirror on the wall of a room, everything in that room that doesn't show a reflection will be a vampire. That's how you test for them."

The hatstand considered this carefully. "I can think of one thing that will never be reflected in that mirror…"

"Oh yes?" replied the table. "What's that, then?"

"The mirror itself," said the hatstand.

There was a brief pause. It lasted two sentences.

"That means…" began the table.

"Yes it does!" bellowed the hatstand in alarm.

"All mirrors are vampires!"

¶ It's true. And that's why people who spend a lot of time in front of a mirror are called 'vein'.

115 MIDDLE OF THE ROAD

The traffic lights said to the roundabout, "Tell me about the latest holiday option for the busy city worker."

"It's called the Traffic Island Break," said the roundabout. "The idea is that a fortnight on a roundabout like me can be as rewarding as one spent on a South Sea atoll. The trips are organised by former financial advisor, Keith Lock, who was stranded on a plot of wasteland in Cardiff when his car suffered a blowout on the exit lane of the Gabalfa interchange. Despite frantic attempts to summon help from passing motorists, Lock was ignored and had to resign himself to a Robinson Crusoe existence on the urban islet. Amid the hardships of surviving in this barren environment, he discovered a sort of peace."

"I wonder how he managed that?" cried the traffic lights.

"He thought the speeding vehicles were like waves," answered the roundabout proudly. "It was very soothing. But more than that, it was intensely real. Returning to his primitive origins made him realise that his entire business life was nothing more than an escapist fantasy."

"What happened afterwards?" persisted the traffic lights.

"Eventually rescued and reunited with his wife, Lock found himself missing the solitude and brambles. He wanted to return as quickly as possible and he decided others should have a chance of sharing the experience. So with the support of his spouse, Lock resigned his job and started his own travel agency. At first, his bank manager was sceptical, but after Lock escorted him on a tour of central reservations, he was persuaded to authorise a loan. Lock rented a traffic island in central Cardiff and within a week was receiving his first customers."

"What kind of holiday do they get?"

"Well, once dropped on the island, contact with the outside world is impossible, so prospective maroons are issued with standard survival equipment: eight music albums of their choice and a few books. Many try to smuggle in jars of coffee. Some of Lock's customers have reported odd occurrences

103

during their periods of isolation. One tourist claimed to have discovered the indigenous inhabitants of the island, a cannibal race with headwear woven from windscreen wipers."

¶ The average employee still prefers Spain and Greece.

116 THE WARLORD

A warlord spent all his pocket money on tubes and jars of tomato purée. Because he was a warlord he had very big pockets made from chain mail, so that he could keep maces, knives and hand-axes in them without fear of the sharp spikes and blades making a hole in the fabric and falling out and landing on his foot and injuring it.

Because his pockets were so large, his pocket money was considerable and he was able to purchase enormous amounts of tomato purée. At home he filled ice-trays with the purée and froze them in his freezer until he had many blocks of frozen concentrated tomato pulp. With these blocks, each of which resembled a little brick, he constructed a building at the bottom of the garden. It was a small building with only one room and he used it as storage space for all his garden tools.

A roving peacemonger came to visit him. "What are you doing?" he asked in astonishment, when he saw the tomato purée house, which was beginning to sag in the heat of the sun.

"I'm a warlord," said the warlord, "and I read in a book of history that in order to be a genuine warlord, one must *shed* blood. I don't particularly like blood, so I'm using tomato purée instead. I might shed other kinds of vegetable juices too, if I have the time."

¶ Bash two tomatoes together and you don't get the sound of tom-toms but just a sticky mess. You can still dance to it, though!

117 THE SAME BOAT

The windmill known as Sessile Beady Mill was still bored with turning in the wind and doing nothing else all day. In fact he was more bored than ever. A sentient hot-air balloon happened to be passing and Sessile called up, "Lucky you! You are free and I bet you have an interesting life. My ambition is to be a film director but I don't see how that dream of mine will ever come true. I'm stuck here."

"Count your blessings," said the balloon with a sigh. "My dream is to be a hairdresser but it'll never happen! I'm not allowed to handle scissors because of my fragile canopy and I don't have arms. Plus I'm allergic to adjustable chairs. It's frankly a shame."

"So we're in the same boat then?" cried Sessile.

"I guess we must be," said the balloon.

Sessile and the balloon looked down and saw that they were standing on the deck of a ship caught in a storm. This was the 'same boat' they were in. They both felt very sick. But the sea wasn't sympathetic at all. In fact it was made of dismissive hands.

¶ The sick is greener on the other side.

118 THE SNOB

An elephant that was fond of practical jokes sniffed a lens up his trunk as far as it would go, then he fixed another lens to the opening of his trunk. One was a convex lens, the other concave, but I don't know which was which. I could find out but frankly I can't be bothered. Anyway, once the lenses were in position, the elephant persuaded an ant to climb inside his throat and take up position at the point where the trunk internally joined the windpipe. Then the elephant straightened his trunk and pointed it at an aardvark that was ambling along.

"What am I supposed to do?" asked the ant.

"I've turned my trunk into a telescope," the elephant explained, "and you are now my astronomer royal. Think of this telescope, in other words my trunk, in other words my nose, as your own. Please refer to it as if it's yours. Seriously, that's what I want."

A sentient hot-air balloon happened to be passing. It had drifted out of the preceding fable thanks to an unexpected breeze. "What are you doing to that poor long-nosed creature that has jam on its nose? Apricot jam, I believe it is," cried the balloon primly.

"I don't have jam on my nose!" protested the elephant.

"When I said 'long-nosed creature' I didn't mean you, but that other long-nosed creature," said the balloon.

"I'm an aardvark," specified the aardvark.

"In that case, what are you doing to that aardvark?" insisted the hot-air balloon, hovering above the elephant.

"Ask the ant inside my throat," answered the elephant; and then with a wink, he added in a whisper, "He's a snob. Even though he's only an ant and very tiny, he has elitist attitudes."

"I *will* ask the ant in your throat!" cried the balloon.

And that's exactly what he did.

The ant's reply was barely audible. "What am I doing to this aardvark? Why, I'm looking down my nose at it!"

¶ Elephants have two nostrils just like us. So the trunk must have been turned into binoculars, not a telescope.

119 A CLOSE BRUSH

A tub of paint had been left lying open. A passing police car stopped and an armed cop inside cried, "Hey you!"

"What's the problem, officer?" stammered the paint.

"Up against the wall, buddy!"

"I can't do that by myself. You'll have to get out, pick up the tub I'm in and fling me blindly at the vertical surface. I'll probably drip down in a variety of mildly aesthetic patterns."

"Fling you? I'm not a goddam abstract expressionist!"

"In that case, use a roller."

"I don't have one. I'm not a goddam housewife!"

"I'm out of suggestions…"

The cop sneered and drove away. The night passed, and the following morning the artist who owned the tub came back. "Sorry for leaving you here! I went to a café and got drunk on absinthe and other beverages that are favoured by bohemians. I hope nothing bad happened in my absence? Did you have a brush with the law?"

"A brush! I forgot that one!" cried the paint.

¶ The paint's name was Hue.

120 TRYING IT ON

A man went into a shop that sold second-hand clothes. He browsed for a long time before picking up a tweed jacket. "Are you interested in that item of clothing?" the assistant asked.

The man frowned at her. "I'm not really sure."

"It thinks it's the most stylish item of clothing in the wardrobe and that it's bound to win all the awards this year," added the assistant, batting her eyelashes. She was an attractive woman.

"May I try it on first?" asked the man hopefully.

"Of course!" said the assistant.

The man approached her and began fondling her breasts.

"Get off, you creep!" she cried.

The man was bewildered. He stepped back with a red face. "I thought you gave me permission to 'try it on'."

"The jacket, not me!" bellowed the assistant.

"I'm deeply sorry," said the man. He approached the jacket and began fondling the breast pockets. "Oh yes!"

"Get off, you creep! I'm male!" cried the jacket.

¶ There were pencils in those pockets.

121 TABLE TALK

A new restaurant was established and the tables were given some time to get to know each other before the first customers arrived. "Why are we all nude?" one of the tables wanted to know.

"We're waiting to get laid," answered a joker.

"Don't be so puerile!" chided a more serious table. "No, the real truth is that the restaurant owners can't afford tablecloths. When we're covered with food, we'll feel less self-conscious."

The tables began chatting.

"Anyone worked in a restaurant before?"

"I did a stint in a café."

"Nice legs! Did you get them waxed?"

"I'm actually foldable."

"We're on castors. Means we can turn the tables on anyone who wants to argue with us. Often we do!"

"I'm made of pine…"

The front door suddenly flew open.

And the first customers came inside. A pig, a waffle, a box, a chump, a resentment, a caterpillar, a gift, a loom, a cuttlefish, an aurora borealis, a duvet, a chair, a sunken continent, a cup that runneth over, an ancient paradox, a snivel, a bone, a toothless cog, a piecrust, a passionate kiss, an aching thigh, a broken

109

window, a phantom, a cat, a bathtub, a chimney clogged with twigs, a forced laugh...

"There are so many of them!" wailed a table.

True enough. And still they came.

...a chewed pencil, a beetroot stain, a vague feeling, a hovercraft, an argument, a dog, an example of jargon, a butterfly, an interpolation, a grotesque fiend, a coconut shy, a confident papaya and a thousand other things... "Far too many! I'm scared!"

"Don't worry," said a table with more experience. "I'm sure the waiter will find an excuse to get rid of them."

¶ If you were paying attention earlier, you'll know what it was.

122 THE INTERNATIONAL PUNFEST

A suburban bungalow somewhere in England. A comfortable lounge with a sofa and a man sat upon it. A woman at a desk in a corner was spinning a globe of planet Earth and frowning at the countries that flew past. Then she opened her mouth to speak.

"Uzbekistan," said Anna.

"I don't know. Who is she?" replied Stan.

"Turkey," added Anna.

"Well, if you already knew that Becky is a turkey, why did you ask me who she was?" grumbled Stan.

"Chile," said Anna.

"Maybe she needs a blanket?"

"Hungary."

"And a bowl of soup."

"Korea."

"She's a turkey, you said. But that's more of a lifestyle than an actual career. Anyway, I don't think it's important. I am more concerned about my own career and lack of income."

"Sudan."

"Why should I? He used to be my best friend. There must be better ways of getting money than that. Maybe your friend Caroline has some financial advice for me?"

"Alaska."

"Please do. She's very knowledgeable about many things. I don't like her cooking very much, though."

"Greece."

"Too much. She fries every meal. I'm no better and what's good for the goose is good for the—"

"Uganda."

"No, I'm not the gander. I'm the goose!"

"Yemen."

"Far out! Groovy baby!"

"Romania."

"Not really. I regret only the depression."

¶ Travel doesn't always broaden the mind, especially armchair travel.

123 A LINEAR ADVENTURE

There was once a line called X who was always very cross. He was tired of being cross all the time, so he went to consult Y, a philosophical line, who told him, "It's just your nature to be cross, there's nothing U or I can do about it. Accept your condition."

"Who are U and I?" wondered X.

"There are also philosophical lines, but untrustworthy."

"I might pay them a visit anyway."

"You'll be wasting your time," warned Y, "but if you really do want a second opinion, ask the Equator."

"Why should I do that?" asked X.

"The Equator is the most widely-travelled line of all. He encircles the entire planet at its widest point."

"What does he do that for? Is he a belt?" asked X.

"With that disrespectful comment, you've crossed the line!" huffed Y, who didn't have a sense of humour.

"But I haven't set off yet!" protested X.

¶ Zzzzzzzzzzzzzzzzz

124 THE MIDAIR MEETING

Two boomerangs met in midair. They were polite to each other. "How do you do?" said one of them. "Pleased to make your acquaintance!" replied the other. Then there was a brief pause.

"Well, I must be getting back now," said the first.

"Me too," added the second.

"I've got an idea," said the first boomerang, who was mischievous and liked to play practical jokes. "Why don't we swap owners? They'll never be able to tell the difference. Instead of turning around at this point, you keep going forward and I'll do the same; and we'll end up in the hands of new people. That might be a laugh."

"I've got an even better idea," retorted the second boomerang. "Why don't we fall in love and get married?"

"I bet that's what they're hoping we'll do! I prefer my own idea. I enjoy fooling humans: it's great fun!"

And so they both continued in a straight line and were caught by hands that hadn't thrown them. The owners of those hands looked glumly down at the lengths of curved wood and said, "Releasing them into boomerang society hasn't worked in the way we anticipated. They didn't meet a mate but changed identity instead. Weird!"

¶ Better not to go straight if you're bent.

125 THROWING A MERINGUE

A philosopher began throwing meringues into the air. Every time he did so, they splattered on the ground. A squirrel who was watching him was bemused and finally asked, "What are you doing? That's such a waste of confectionary! Give them to me if you don't want them. You must be a Welsh philosopher if you're so daft!"

"I am indeed a Welsh philosopher," said the philosopher, "and the day after tomorrow I have to travel on a train from Swansea to Tenby; but in the meantime I am testing the theory that if you throw a meringue into the air it will always come back to you."

The squirrel shook his head. "An ordinary meringue will never do that. It must be a *frightened* meringue."

113

The philosopher looked at the meringue he held in his hand. It was his last one. "How shall I frighten it?"

"Shout 'Boo!' at it, of course!" said the squirrel.

The philosopher did that and then he hurled the meringue at the squirrel. He thought the squirrel was mocking him and he planned for the meringue to splatter the furry creature's face as a punishment. But the meringue tuned in midair at the halfway point and flew back at increasing velocity and exploded in the philosopher's visage, smearing it with sticky matter and dripping in gloops onto his shirt.

¶ Boo meringue.

126 THE EQUATOR'S MISTAKE

The Greenwich Meridian said to the Equator, "Why have you dressed up in that ridiculous outfit? Four paws, a tail, a golden mane and long teeth! I can't see any good reason for it."

"I'm expressing what I really am," came the reply.

"But you're the Equator! That's what you really are. I wonder who has been filling your head — not that you have one —with such rubbish? Did you read one of those books again?"

"Yes I did. It was an encyclopaedia. And it told me that the Equator is an 'imaginary lion that runs around the world'. Now I'm off for my first run of infinity. See you on each lap!"

¶ Line, not lion, you fool!

127 THE BED'S ERROR

A kettle was feeling anxious. "My master usually comes at this time to boil me for a cup of coffee. I wonder what's the matter with him? I hope he's not ill or injured or something!"

And it shouted out the name 'Kevin' as loudly as it could. But the bed in the bedroom called back, "Hush! Don't disturb him. He told me that he was going to spend the entire morning with a beast that has four paws, a tail, a golden mane and long teeth."

"Why would he want to do that?" gasped the kettle.

"I don't know," admitted the bed, "but I definitely heard him say last night that he intended to have a lion."

¶ Lie-in, not lion, you fool!

128 THE DISAPPOINTING MERMAID

A man with a very long beard saw a woman floundering about in a pond, so he kneeled right on the water's edge and tied a slipknot in the end of his beard and turned it into a lasso; then he snared the woman and pulled her safely to shore. He gasped.

"You are very beautiful. You must be a princess."

She blushed. "I'm a mere maid."

He gasped. "A mermaid? Where's your tail?"

"My tale?" cried the woman. "Are you sure you want to hear it? Most people I meet screw up their faces and put their hands over their ears and cry out in anguish when I start telling my tale. It's very long, you see. In fact it takes at least seventeen hours to reach the conclusion. I was born in the cottage of my parents and from an early age I wanted to learn how to communicate with the flowers—"

¶ Two hours later he threw her back in…

129 RHINO COP

A rhinoceros joined the police force. They told him, "First you arrest the criminals and then you charge them."

He nodded and went off to tackle crime in the big city. He saw a man sexually molesting a poor cabbage in a greengrocer's and he shouted out that the fellow was under arrest.

"But I was just testing its firmness!" the man replied.

"You're under arrest anyway," the rhino said.

"On what charge?" demanded the man.

"On this one!" bellowed the rhino as he charged him.

The poor cabbage was rescued…

Later, back at the police station, the rhino said, "I had a busy first day at work. I arrested ten criminals and charged all of them, but now there's no room left on my horn and the blood is trickling into my eyes. Will you remove them for me? Much appreciated!"

¶ Take care when you mishandle cabbages.

130 THE HIPPOCRATIC OATH

There was a hippopotamus who studied medicine and became a doctor. A sickly owl summoned him to his perch and said, "I have a fever. I think I might have contracted malaria."

"Can't you come down here?" asked the hippo.

"No, I'm too ill to move!"

"Then I'll have to try and climb that tree and inch myself along those thin branches to reach you," said the hippo.

And so he began climbing the tree. But, halfway along a branch, there was a snapping noise and he plummeted back down to the ground, where he landed with a very heavy thud.

"Shit! Bugger! Bloody!" the hippo roared.

"I didn't know doctors were allowed to use bad language," remarked the owl in some considerable surprise.

"Only if they are hippos," explained the hippo.

"Ah, that's the meaning of the Hippocratic oath!" cried the owl.

"Yes indeed. How do you feel now?"

"Much better, thanks."

¶ It wasn't malaria. Just a head cold.

131 CAN'T THINK OF A TITLE

An odd-job man called Tim was in the habit of wandering the land with a fish in a bowl of salt water.

One day he met a duck, melon and anecdote coming towards him on a lonely road.

"Anything interesting in that direction?" he asked.

"Not really," they said.

"Nothing at all? I find that hard to believe!"

"Just a pickle jar by the name of Boris," they answered. "What about in your direction? Is it worth continuing to where you've come from? We don't have a map between us, you see."

"A rhino policeman lives that way," warned Tim.

"Oh dear," they commented.

"We're stuck, aren't we," said Tim gloomily.

"Yes, in a rubbish fable!"

¶ It's over now, thank goodness…

132 POOR VISIBILITY

A gorgon was driving her Jaguar through the pouring rain. The Jaguar was growling and grumbling because cats don't like water. "Why don't you stop at the next settlement and find shelter?" he asked. "If you keep going, you'll be certain to crash."

"Crash? Why should I do that?" asked the gorgon.

"Because of the poor visibility!"

"No need for you to worry about that!" answered the gorgon. "I've got a set of windscreen vipers on my head."

¶ She did crash later, funnily enough.

133 THE GENEROUS BREASTS

"I have very generous breasts," said the whore.

"Really?" cried the wolf.

"Try them for yourself if you don't believe me."

"Fair enough, I will!" announced the wolf. He leaned closer and rested his long nose in her exposed cleavage.

"Will you give me one hundred dollars?" he asked.

"We're not *that* generous!" cried the breasts.

"How about fifty?" the wolf persisted.

The breasts discussed the matter with each other. "No, we've decided to become stingy instead. It's easier."

The wolf went on his way, tail between his legs.

The whore sighed as she returned to work.

"I have very stingy breasts. Extremely stingy!" she called to her next potential client. "Skinflint nipples too."

¶ If prostitution is really the oldest profession, how did men earn the money to visit brothels, unless—?

134 THE NEW KNIGHT

"I've not seen you at Camelot before," said Sir Galahad.

"That's right," answered the new knight, "I'm just doing a one-off job for King Arthur. He has started using workers who aren't affiliated with the Round Table. I'm one of those."

"Oh, I see," sniffed Sir Galahad. "And you are Sir—?"

"Freelancealot," came the reply.

¶ Inventing morals for these fables is getting a bit boring now.

135 THE NATURAL SPECTACLE

A raccoon said, "Help me roll this giant circle of crystal over to one side of that headland, if you'd be so kind."

The grizzly bear did so. "Now help me roll this second giant circle of crystal to the other side," added the raccoon. The bear did that also. It was hard work, but he didn't complain.

When he had finished, the raccoon asked him, "Do you think that this headland looks like an enormous nose?"

"I do," agreed the bear, "but what's the point of asking me to do what you did? Have you wasted my time?"

"By no means," replied the raccoon. "I am merely trying to encourage more tourists to the area. It was devoid of any incredible scenery, but now it has a remarkable natural spectacle."

¶ The crystals were quartz. I saw you through them reading this fable. Don't pretend you weren't!

136 ON THE SHELF

"Help! I've been left on the shelf!"

"But what are you?" cried the anxious woodlouse.

"A spare shelf," said the spare shelf.

"Fancy keeping a shelf on a shelf!" marvelled the woodlouse.

¶ I don't fancy it, sorry.

137 THE FAMOUS ALEXANDER

"I am famous! I am the best! I am Alexander!"

"Alexander the Great?" cried the anxious woodlouse.

"No. Alexander the Technique!"

"Bah! You're such a poseur!" sniffed the woodlouse.

¶ I sniffed a woodlouse once.

138 BOULDER CROQUET

A foghorn that was braver than others of his kind blew himself as loud as he could when he saw a cloud with alternative leanings massing on the horizon. "What did you do that for?" asked the cloud. "I'm not a hazard to shipping. I'm just a ball of fluff!"

"How can I be sure of that?" retorted the foghorn. "For all I know you may be concealing a clutch of continents laid by a tectonic plate. What if those baby landmasses roll out of their aerial nest and fall on commercial vessels plying the waters beneath?"

"That's a slander! I'm harmless. Look! Here comes a ship now. Let's ask the passengers if I'm a danger..."

The ship was a longboat and it contained a gnome and a Viking. "Do you mind if I ask you a question?" the cloud said as they passed below it with the wind in their single large sail.

"Go ahead. But make it quick. We're playing deck croquet and don't wish to be disturbed," said the Viking.

"Would you say I was a hazard to shipping?"

But the moment the cloud leaned over to ask this question, a handful of eggs rolled out and fell onto the longboat's deck. They were eggs that had been laid by a tectonic plate! They knocked the croquet balls over the side and into the sea, ruining the game.

The Viking was so angry that he picked up the gnome by the feet and swung him like an ancient weapon at the cloud, who retreated in a panic while the foghorn sighed superciliously.

¶ There's no mace like gnome.

139 ANTIMATTER PASTA

The astronomer removed his eye from the telescope. "I have got some startling news! The sun is going out!"

"Going out? Going out?" came the shocked response. "This is terrible! A catastrophe! You mean to say that..."

"Yes," replied the astronomer grimly. "It seems that a new restaurant has opened beyond the orbit of Pluto!"

¶ The prices were astronomical, but it had a star chef.

140 THE POLITICO AND THE POLYP

"I hate colonialism!" cried the politico.

"But—" protested the polyp. The politico growled, "What? Do you plan on contradicting me? Are you some sort of secret Fascist? I say that forming colonies is utterly wrong!"

"But—" repeated the polyp. The politico didn't give him a chance to say more than that. He shook with fury.

"The British Empire was founded on the sweat and blood of the poor people of its colonies; the same holds true for the French, Spanish, Dutch, Portuguese, Belgian, Italian and Japanese Empires! Colonialism is wrong and there are no exceptions to this rule!"

The polyp finally managed to speak without being interrupted. "But I'm a polyp and together with my comrades we have created a coral reef. Polyps live in colonies, you see, like so many other lifeforms. Without colonialism, coral reefs wouldn't exist."

"So you think that colonies are a good idea, do you?"

"Why yes, from a personal point of—"

"Then die under the hammer of liberalism!"
shouted the politico, as he violently smashed the
polyp into slime.

¶ Liberals can be too extreme at times.

141 KING OF THE LIARS

"The King of the Beasts is—" began the gazelle.
  "Lion," interrupted the giraffe.
  A zebra happened to be within earshot and cried:
  "Is he? I suppose he is much less successful than
he claims to be? Or maybe he doesn't have half the
strength he pretends to have? Am I on the right track
or are his main falsehoods more in the line of
financial boasts and exaggerated sexual prowess?"
  There was a pause. Then the zebra added:
  "What animal is he anyway?"
  The gazelle and giraffe shook their heads.

¶ Lion, not lying, you fool!

142 THE POPULAR GARDEN PLANT

"The most popular garden plant is—" began the
aphid.
  "Geranium," interrupted the ladybird.
  A hornet happened to be within earshot and cried:
  "Is it? I suppose it's because of the glow? Or
maybe gardeners have a liking for the fact it is an
essential ingredient in nuclear bombs, but why that

should be the case is strange! Perhaps they appreciate that it's heavy and won't blow away in the wind."

There was a pause. Then the hornet added:

"What atomic number is it anyway?"

The aphid and ladybird shook their heads.

¶ Geranium, not uranium, you fool!

143 HOMEOPATHIC CURSES

"I'm a homeopath!" said the homeopath.

"Pleased to meet you," answered Bandit the Badger.

"Listen carefully. One of the principles of homeopathy is that the more something is diluted, the stronger it gets!"

"What's in this jar?" asked Bandit, holding it up.

"Very expensive medicine!"

"Oops! Clumsy me! I just dropped it!"

The jar shattered into shards.

"You black and white idiot! You light and dark moron! You day and night buffoon!" shrieked the homeopath.

"Hold on there a moment," said Bandit calmly. "Those curses aren't very strong. Why don't you make them stronger by diluting them? That way you can be certain of insulting me as much as I deserve. Try diluting them as much as you possibly can..."

The homeopath considered this suggestion.

"Very well. Are you ready?"

"Yes I am," replied Bandit. "Do your worst!"

"You lovely badger! You incredibly nice creature! You fabulous and lovely being! You astounding thing! You darling entity that I adore and worship with all my tenderness..."

"That's much better. This homeopathy is growing on me," declared Bandit as he absorbed the praise.

¶ Don't meddle with medicines you misunderstand!

144 POOR PLATO

"Poor Plato!" said a student of the famous philosopher.

"Are you feeling sorry for him?" asked a sentient hot-air balloon who was passing overhead and heard this.

"Yes, I am," confirmed the student.

"But why? He is renowned and has many devoted disciples who love him. Does he need your sympathy?"

"I think he does," replied the student seriously. "Allow me to explain why. Every kiss or cuddle he ever bestows on anyone, however erotically intense, is always *Platonic* by definition."

¶ Aristotle had a lot on his Plato.

145 THE SEA TRIALS

Captain Dangleglum said, "I have a new ship and I intend to hold some sea trials, but first I need a lawyer."

"I'm one of those!" blurted Tonguewaggle Chipchop.

"Then I leave matters in your hands…"

A few weeks later the trial began. The ship was moored in the dock of the court and the judge was the ocean itself, wearing a wig of spray, who squinted with vast whirlpool eyes and demanded, "Are you the sea-going vessel known as *The Tweed Jacket*?"

"That's me," admitted the ship in question.

"Humph! And is it also true that you openly voted for a hedgehog with the campaign slogan 'I know everything about everything' to become the next president of an earlier fable?"

"I'm afraid I did," answered the ship.

"In that case, I find you guilty of being a floating voter!" boomed the judge, seething under the moon's pull.

"In that case?" echoed the ship. "Which case?"

"This one," specified the judge, indicating a wooden sea chest.

"Good job I'm not inside it then!"

¶ The ship was acquitted. The retrial took place in Hull.

146 HOLDING UP THE RIVER

"Throughout history men have carried women across raging rivers," said the hero to the girl on the slippery bank.

"Funny how history is full of rivers," remarked the girl.

"Um… I didn't mean it like that…"

127

"I find it funny anyway, hilarious in fact!"

"Er... yes, I suppose it is. But today we're going to try something new with this river," commented the hero.

"It's not really a river, is it? More of a brook..."

"No matter. Instead of carrying *you* across *it*, in the traditional fashion, I intend to carry it across you! Ready?"

"Yes, I am. In fact I'm in something of a rush!"

The hero bent down and thrust his strong fingers under the edge of the riverbed. Then he heaved and puffed but only managed to lift the water a few inches high. The girl sighed.

"I'll never fit in that tiny space. Lift it more!"

"I'm trying. It's much heavier than I expected. Give me a few minutes and I'm sure I can get it to head height."

"I can't wait. I will brook no delay!" cried the girl.

¶ The pun doesn't really work, does it?

147 THE ALLOTMENT

The triffid said, "I have an allotment! Now I can grow my own food. Do you want to come along and see it?"

"Sure thing," replied the crow. "Show me..."

"Talking about food," muttered the triffid, "didn't a scarecrow once share part of his lunch with you?"

"Yes, his cheese and olives, but that was ages ago!"

The two companions went to the place where the allotments were. A few other triffids were busy digging the soil. They looked up and nodded a rustic greeting to the newcomers.

"Hello Wynn!" some of them shouted.

"That's my proper name," the triffid confided to the crow.

"What's your surname?" asked the crow.

"Dam," answered the triffid.

"No need to curse, I was only asking!"

"No, that's my full name. Wynn Dam. Hey, take a look over there! An early crop has sprung up already…"

The crow glanced to the spot indicated by the triffid's tendril. A row of humans had pushed through the soil overnight, bald scalps gleaming with fresh dew, eyes blinking slowly.

"They grow fast, that particular strain," remarked the triffid.

"I never knew you could plant humans!"

"Plant humans? What's a plant human? Is it a hybrid between a triffid and a man? I don't like the sound of that!"

¶ Neither did the crow.

148 THE CASTAWAY COOK

Among the survivors of a shipwreck was a cook. He decided to make a meal for all the other marooned individuals. A giant iron pot had washed ashore and he lit a fire under it and boiled seaweed, coconuts and various other plants growing along the shore.

But he didn't have a wooden spoon and had to find another method of stirring the soup. One of the girls among the survivors had lost most of her clothes and her lithe tanned body was almost naked. This sight made the cook feel aroused. Then it occurred to him that he could use the thing that was growing in his trousers to take the place of the wooden spoon. So that's what he, improbably, did.

Some of the other castaways passed the time by playing catch with a spare coconut. One of them threw it too high and it landed in the soup with a splash! The lithe tanned girl said:

"Don't worry! I'll get it back!" And she thrust her arm into the pot of soup and groped around in the liquid.

"Have you found it yet?" called one of the others.

"No," she answered.

"What can you feel in there?"

"An erection stirring," she replied.

"No, it's already at maximum!" objected the cook.

¶ This is probably the worst fable of the entire bunch.

149 DOWN THE SHOPS

"I'm going down the shops," declared the robot. "Can I get you anything while I'm there? Toothpaste? Floss?"

"No thanks," replied the sabre-toothed tiger.

The robot turned to depart…

"Wait a moment!" cried the furry prehistoric beast. "Will you get me a roll of *c'est la vie*? Here's the money."

"*C'est la vie*?" wondered the robot. "What's that?"

"It's French *c'est la tape* for sticking your life back together again. My destiny has just dropped off my soul."

"Ooh, that sounds nasty. I'll be back in half an hour."

"Thanks. Take care on the roads!"

¶ It took the robot forty minutes actually.

150 THE FLYING FISH

A shoal of flying fish was swimming through the ocean. Suddenly one of the fish nearest the front shouted, "Our way forward is blocked by a mass of ice! I never expected such a thing!"

"A mass of ice?" cried one of the more experienced members of the shoal. "Oh, I see what you mean..." His name was Lindy and he held the fish record for the longest solo flight.

"Have you seen this before?" asked the first fish.

"Yes, it's an iceberg," said Lindy.

"Well, let's just fly over it! We *are* flying fish, after all. We can easily re-enter the ocean on the far side."

"Be careful!" Lindy answered.

"What for? I'll go first. It will be simple!"

"Not true," warned Lindy. "You must glide very high when you make the attempt; and so must the fish that follow. Don't you realise that 10% of an iceberg lies *above* the water...?"

¶ This is the final fable in this particular sequence. Bye!

The Parable of the Homeless Fable

It's high time I told you about a homeless fable I once knew. It's always better to tell urgent tales at high time; those raconteurs who tell them at low time or middle time don't seem to appreciate that increased chronic elevation benefits everyone. The views are finer up there, the air fresher. High time is best. And it's high time right now, so I ought to get started while my temporal altimeter is at maximum.

There was a fable that didn't belong to any known collection, neither from antiquity nor more modern times. Whether he was always homeless or had been expelled from some official opus is unknown; he claimed not to recall anything about his origins. I believed him then and I believe him now. I found him wandering, naked and delirious, in the street outside my house in the dark days of a very cold winter.

Naturally I took him in and nursed him back to a semblance of health. I'm not an especially sympathetic individual, my altruism isn't copious or available on tap, but I can feel pity for a sentient entity that clearly has no chance of survival without assistance. So it was my moral duty to help. It can't honestly be asserted that I looked forward to enjoying the company of this fabular foundling when it recovered.

For I am a loner, a misanthrope; and yes, misanthropy can apply to the creations and products of the human race as well as to the race itself. The fable is an artform I regard with distaste, a maudlin package of words that constitutes an item of propaganda. They have often been used to facilitate repression and stasis by advising those who read them

133

to be satisfied with the existing state of affairs, to be submissive.

It is in the interests of the ruling classes, the rich and powerful elite, to foster among the poor the idea that we should all be satisfied with our lot in life, that to strive for change is catastrophic. Most fables encourage this reactionary notion: they warn the underprivileged masses to remain meek and unthreatening. They aren't just harmless little tales but dampeners of ambition, metaphoric blows against progress.

In theory, a wise man shouldn't help an injured fable.

But I am no revolutionary and I care not what regimes humans devise to make their own miserable lives even worse, provided I'm not included in a census of victims. Nonetheless I am an organic being with feelings, a recluse but not one with etiolated emotions; and I vowed to do my best to look after the feverish fable. I put him to bed, kept him warm, sang songs of soothing serenity while he softly slumbered.

Two weeks later, he was better. He sat at the breakfast table with me. I munched my overdone toast, spread thickly with apricot jam, and slurped my sweet black coffee and nodded politely at him and said, "Well now. It still remains to be decided what to do next with you. I have explained that you can't stay here indefinitely. I value my privacy and seclusion and you have already managed to disrupt my routine."

"Thank you for saving my life, Mr Excelsior!" he replied.

I quietly acknowledged his gratitude.

"But I want you to leave this afternoon," I added.

"I have no wish to be a burden, sir!"

We remained silent for several minutes, but there was no awkwardness in the hiatus. I don't think he expected or even hoped I would change my mind; indeed, he seemed rather anxious to be on his way, but not because he was the roving type, like a rumour, wandering from ear to ear, brain to brain, never pinned to the printed page. On the contrary, he had a mission to get himself lodged in a book. I realised that.

A homeless fable, it occurred to me, wasn't a real fable, any more than an approximation is a fact. On some deep thematic level he had a burning urge to secure a place in an appropriate text, to insert himself into a tome where he might flourish and reach his full potential; and it seemed I ought to aid him in this quest also. Otherwise the charity I had already expended on him would be wasted, for he would wither.

"Very well," I said briskly. "We must find you a proper home."

"Thank you kindly, Mr Excelsior."

"The logical place to search is in my library."

And that's where we went, when my final slice of toast was gone and the jam spoon licked as clean as a table's soul. There was a shelf of dusty volumes that were mostly collections of fables. Like a protective father, I held hands with the fable as I knocked on the spine of the first title in the line of bound books. Most of them hadn't been consulted for decades and were cobwebbed with spiders' domiciles.

A voice rasped, "Yes? Who is there? What do you want?"

"Do you have any room for a lost fable?"

"Are you playing a joke?"

"Absolutely not! It's a simple question."

"But don't you know who I am? I'm a definitive selection of Aesop's fables, the most historically prestigious of all such collections! Scholars have ratified my entire contents over generations and they can't possibly be adjusted now. It's beyond consideration!"

I didn't bother arguing but moved along to the next book.

"Hello?" called another voice.

"Will you kindly take in this homeless fable?"

"No. I'm the *Panchatantra*, attributed to Vishnu Sharma and older than two thousand years. Your fable is not even of the correct ethnicity. Your request is ludicrous and perhaps offensive!"

I proceeded to the third book in the row but the outcome was the same. The fourth, fifth, sixth and seventh volumes were even more disdainful in their utter refusal to contemplate adopting the fable whose prosaic grip on my hand weakened with each rejection. The collection of fables gathered by the Roman writer called Hyginus at least had the common decency to offer apologies for his rebuttal of our plea.

His near contemporary, Phaedrus, was downright rude; but possibly I knocked a little too hard on his spine, which was breaking apart with age. These were very conservative and hallowed works and petitioning them to expand their table of contents was patently absurd; and yet I had given them free shelf space for many years and I had hoped one of them would be willing to overlook tradition if I asked.

True, the relatively obscure volume attributed to Vardan Aygektsi, the 13th Century Armenian fabulist, did deign to discuss the grim plight of the homeless fable with me for a few minutes.

"Does he feature animals, that vagrant of yours?"

I was stumped by his question. "I don't know. Let me check. I haven't actually read him yet, I'm afraid."

"Humph! Then you're hardly in a position to recommend him to me, are you? Well, hurry and find out!"

"Do you feature animals?" I asked the homeless fable.

"I don't think so," he replied.

"What do you mean by that?" I cried. "Don't you know what happens in your own narrative? Impossible!"

"Fables aren't in the habit of reading themselves."

"But surely some of the characters inside your text can do the reading for you and let you know?" I persisted.

"Their eyes will point outwards, unless they turn around, and that will only happen if they are fleeing danger."

"So there is no danger in your tale? That's a start!"

"Or else no characters," he added.

"A fable without any characters!" I groaned.

"Or possibly they *do* exist and they *are* in danger, but the danger is too great for them to stop and read anything. They are too busy fleeing," said Vardan Aygektsi's softly rustling pages.

I nodded at this suggestion; it was plausible.

"Whatever the facts, I cannot read myself," insisted the fable.

I rubbed my chin furiously in response.

But his excuse was valid. So I finally decided to read him and find out the truth for myself. I was mildly shocked by what I discovered when I peered inside him, but I have a strong mental constitution and recovered my composure rapidly. I am not easily intimidated by self-referentiality, recursion, loops, twists and hyperspatial geometries; indeed, the house in which I dwell is a whitewashed tesseract.

"There are no animals inside you," I declared.

Vardan Aygektsi snorted; perhaps the book was sneezing on its thick dust, in the same way that an octopus might tickle itself senseless. With a heavy heart, I led the fable away from the shelf of books. It was pointless continuing our quest here. The columns of untried fabulists retreated into the distance: Berechiah, Biernat, Krasicki, Lessing, De la Fontaine (most elegant of all), Samaniego, Florian, Krylov.

None would accept the homeless fable. I knew this.

As we returned to the kitchen, my hapless charge asked, "No animals at all? Not even human beings?"

"There is a man. Just one though," I sighed.

"With inanimate objects?"

"Yes, you are that kind of fable," I said.

"Do they speak in words?"

I nodded. "Yes, they do. In a contrived manner."

"Spoons, chairs, clouds?"

"No, not them. I will explain soon."

We reached the kitchen. I brewed more coffee. Then I sat the fable on my callused knee and began, "You are an example of what is often called metafiction. In other words you are a fiction that makes overt reference to its fictional status as an integral part of its own text. Indeed, you reference yourself in a tight loop. Your opening words are, '*It's high time I told you about a homeless fable I once knew.*' So—"

He blinked up at me. "What?"

I extended my hands in a gesture of surrender to fate. "In our present culture, there is no literary form more unjustly maligned than metafiction. Readers will say you are too clever for your own good; that you are smug and shallow, that you are merely showing off. Such insults won't hurt less for being ill-judged. Your life will become a perfect misery. It's my duty to protect you from that. I have an idea."

He looked up at me and trembled, but there was strength in his gaze, a determination not to appear weak.

"I will embed you in a parable," I declared.

"A parable?" he muttered.

"Yes, with a moral to the effect that we must be kinder to the products of metafiction, more considerate of self-referentiality. Parables are always about ordinary men and women, never animals or inanimate objects, and that's how they differ by definition from fables; if you are embedded in a parable, the focus of your story will shift from you, a talking fable, to me, a man; a man who makes a plea for you."

He looked uncertain. "Are parables comfortable?"

I slurped my coffee loudly, one of my talents. "They tend to be small and cramped, but don't worry. The parable won't be your home. You will live in the minds of the readers who read *this* story, the tale I am currently writing for you, the actual parable that is a vehicle to carry you from non-existence into living brains. The instant the parable is published you must be ready to leap out from the page…"

"Will I have a soft landing?" he whispered.

"Oh yes! Brains are spongy and will absorb the impact. You will find your new abode roomy and furnished with taste. You can ask for no finer home than the brain of a good reader."

"At what point should I make the leap?" he asked.

"When they reach this point."

"Now?" he babbled.

"Now!" I cried; and he sprang out...

...and landed in *your* consciousness. Did you feel him bounce off your synapses with a slight thud? I know that he'll be happy there among your other thoughts, your memories and feelings. Your brain is one of the best to be found anywhere; thus I thank you from the top of the bottom of my heart. If I can ever return the favour, let me know. Regards to you! Please write your name in the following space.

```
┌─────────────────────────────────┐
│                                 │
│                                 │
│                                 │
└─────────────────────────────────┘
```

Rhysop's Return

57 Varieties of Daftness

1 DUCK IN DISGUISE

A curious duck disguised itself as a human and went off to the big city to see what life was like there. He nodded politely at everyone he passed in the street and said, "Good morning." And the people always responded to him as if he was a real human being.

The duck knew that his disguise was effective and he felt pleased with himself. In the afternoon he went to the park to feed the ducks, which was very ironic and thus amusing. Then in the early evening he visited a pub and drank several pints of strong beer.

"Pretending to be human is easy. No one suspects the truth!" he said to himself in glee as he waddled out of the pub. Next he went to the nearest fashionable theatre, bought a ticket and saw a play. The play was about a goat that was stuck at the top of a cliff.

The actor who played the goat was a sheep and she wasn't much good, so the duck left the theatre early and strolled casually down the alleyways of an area called the Red Light District.

But now when he called out a greeting to other pedestrians, they were embarrassed and looked away. In a shadowy doorway directly ahead was a woman wearing a very short skirt. Her legs were sheathed in stockings and her cleavage was brazenly exposed.

"What can I do for you, ducky?" she lisped at him.

The duck was so shocked he quacked.

It was now too late to keep up the pretence. So he turned and waddled away as fast as he could. "Of all of them in this vast metropolis," he told himself, "only *she* is smart. But why?"

¶ Because she's a whore unto herself. That's my guess.

2 THE BOMB SCARE

A man wanted to go to his favourite coffee shop during his lunch hour but the police had sealed off the street.

"What's going on?" he asked a nearby officer.

"There's been a bomb scare!" came the reply.

The man tried to peer through the cordon to see for himself. "But how did that happen?" he asked nervously, because he realised that the bomb must be right outside his coffee shop.

The policeman answered, "The bomb was sauntering along innocently enough when suddenly a ghost jumped out from nowhere and frightened it. The poor thing's a nervous wreck."

The man stood on tiptoes and now he could see the bomb shaking and sobbing in the street. A man in a padded camouflage jacket was patting it gently and offering it a cup of sweet tea.

"Luckily the bomb squad got here quickly," the policeman said, "and I am confident they'll soon calm it down."

The man snorted in anger. "What's the world coming to? Those ghosts ought to be ashamed of themselves, scaring a harmless bomb like that for no reason. They should be locked up!"

"We tried that a few times, but they just float out through the walls. I blame the parents," said the policeman.

"But do ghosts have parents?"

"The cadavers then. That's who I blame!"

¶ Can ghosts understand body language? And if so, how?

3 THE FRUITY ALCOHOLIC BEVERAGE

A polecat decided to throw a party for all his friends. On the morning of the occasion he went into the forest and gathered as many kinds of fruit as he could, including apples, pears, plums, peaches, kumquats, bananas and pineapples. Then he chopped them up, threw them into an enormous bowl and poured in bottles of rum and brandy.

When the first guests arrived he ladled some of this brew into glasses for them. It was powerful stuff and they were soon rather tipsy. More and more guests arrived and everyone had a really enjoyable time. There was music and laughter and dancing, and even, for those who like that kind of thing, plenty of howling at the full moon.

But things got out of hand when one of the drunken squirrels snatched a lighted candelabrum and ran with it up a tree. The wax dripped down on the heads of some of the other animals. "Stop that!" cried the polecat who was the host, but the squirrel ignored him.

"Let me try!" suggested a bear, and he roared up at the squirrel: "What are you doing? You'll set the tree on fire!"

But the squirrel gave an incomprehensible reply.

This made the bear angry. "Come down here at once or I'll punch your lights out!" he bellowed in a fierce voice.

The squirrel blew a slobbery kiss and giggled.

"I warned you!" cried the bear.

"Are you really going to punch his lights *out*?" gasped a worried raven who was a close friend of the squirrel.

"Too right I am! Watch this!" growled the bear as he stormed over to the table where the bowl was located.

With the polecat's ladle he filled his glass to the brim with the fruity alcoholic beverage and then he came back and flicked his paw so that the contents were flung upwards into the tree.

The liquid splashed over the squirrel and the candelabrum but instead of extinguishing the flames it made them flare up as the rum and brandy in the mixture ignited. The raven said:

"Oh no! You punched his lights *up* by mistake!"

¶ There were polecat dancers in the adjacent clearing. The neighbours complained but no action was taken.

4 THE MAGICAL EYE

There was a magical eye that didn't belong to any head. It just rolled over the ground and played tricks. "I bet I'm more magical than you," it said to a genie it met on a beach one morning.

The tide had washed the bottle containing the genie onto the sands and left it there. The genie was willing to accept the eye's challenge. "I am an outstanding genie and I'm able to transform myself into any object just by thinking about it. Can you do that too?"

"Yes, I can," said the eye. "Watch this!" And it changed itself into one of those mechanical devices that lift heavy weights into the air. The genie scowled and copied him. "That's very simple!" he chortled. So now there were two of those devices on the beach.

"Well then," said the eye. "Try this for size!" And it turned into one of those tools with teeth that are used to cut through wood. The genie wasn't impressed and he too became an identical copy of the same tool. "Child's play!" he rasped in considerable derision.

"How about this?" cried the eye. And it transformed itself into a horse chestnut minus the spiky casing, but not an ordinary chestnut of that type. No, it had a hole drilled through it and it dangled from a string. The genie had to admit defeat. "I can't match that."

The magical eye was triumphant. "Then I am the best, I am the king, I am the Caesar of shapeshifters, yes I am!"

The genie was confused. "Why the *Caesar*?" he asked.

The answer was as follows:
"Eye crane, eye saw, eye conker!"

¶ I'll just get my quote and leave…

5 THE COUGH

An aardvark went to visit a baboon that was an old friend from university days. They had both studied *humanology*, learning about those weird and illogical beasts called 'men' and 'women'. When the aardvark arrived at the baboon's house, he was surprised to be met by an anxious doctor. The doctor, who was a meerkat, said in a low voice, "Have you come to visit Toby? I'm sorry to say he has been ill."

The aardvark was worried. "In that case, why aren't you attending to him? Why are you out here in the sun?"

"I can't stand the coughing," replied the doctor.

The aardvark was horrified.

"You can't stand the coffin? They gave him an ugly coffin! This is a terrible outcome! He was so ill that he died and they put him in a coffin his own doctor can't bear to look at?"

The doctor laughed. "You misunderstand me. I didn't say 'coffin' but 'coughing'. I can't stand the coughing."

The aardvark sighed in relief. "Thank goodness!"

The doctor scrutinised him. "Incidentally, you have some apricot jam on your nose. Are you aware of that?"

"Yes, yes," cried the aardvark, "but let me get past now. I want to see Toby and commiserate with him."

"That won't do much good," said the doctor.

The aardvark ignored these words and squeezed past into the house. A passageway led to the baboon's bedroom. The aardvark entered and to his amazement saw a coffin lying on the bed. The lid was swinging open and shut and every time it did so, it coughed.

The doctor came up behind him. "Toby died a couple of days ago but they put him in a coffin that is very sick. The coffin is quite ugly but that doesn't trouble me; it's the coughing I can't stand! I wish the carpenters would return to nail down the lid..."

¶ Words that have the same pronunciation as each other but different spellings and meanings are called 'homophones'. Or in the case of this particular fable, 'baboonophones'.

6 THE BEANS

A jackdaw who was flying over an allotment with his friend happened to glance down and see a plot where broad beans were growing. "Look at dem broads!" he remarked as he pointed with a claw. The other jackdaw frowned and said, "Very tasty, I'm sure. But why do you persist in using a fake Brooklyn accent? It's annoying."

"Sorry," replied the first jackdaw. He kept his beak shut but the effort was too much. "Do you have a light, mac?"

The second jackdaw sighed. "Only a heavy raincoat."

"I've heard that joke before," said the woman down below who owned the plot of land where the broad beans grew. She watched the birds depart and then she continued to search for her own friend, whom she had lost a few hours ago. "Where are you, Marge?"

She wandered out of her own plot, away from the broad beans and into a region of the allotment where other kinds of beans grew. And she kept calling for her friend. "Marge! Marge!"

One of the new bean patches overheard her and was offended. "Marge indeed! How dare you? We are *butter*beans!"

¶ I've bean meaning to tell this fable for ages.

7 A LOT ON HIS PLATYPUS

A platypus was sitting in the bath when his doorbell rang, so he got out of the tub and went to answer it. A wolverine stood there and said, "I am a debt collector and I'm here to make sure you pay an overdue bill. I won't leave until you give me the cash."

"I don't owe anyone anything!" objected the platypus.

"That's not what it says here."

"Says *where*?" insisted the platypus.

And the wolverine held up an official looking document. "This is a bill for five hundred euros. Pay me now!"

"But what's it a bill *for*?" demanded the platypus.

"A prostitute you encountered in an alleyway in the Red Light District of a city after going to a pub and theatre."

"That wasn't me!" cried the platypus. "That was a duck six fables ago! Why should I pay on his behalf?"

The wolverine sneered. "It's your responsibility."

"But how? I don't understand."

"Easy. Because you're a *duck billed* platypus."

¶ The prostitute's name was Marge.

8 AN ANGRY CONDIMENT

A bell pepper went on holiday with a pinch of salt. After they settled into the hotel, they began unpacking. "I don't believe this!" cried the pinch of salt. "You forgot the toothpaste!"

"I didn't forget. I deliberately neglected to bring it."

"But why? Are you an idiot?"

The bell pepper said, "We don't have any teeth, so what's the point of taking along tubes of toothpaste?"

The pinch of salt wasn't pacified and roared:

"When normal couples go on vacation they always pack hygiene items in their luggage! You bulbous lout!"

"But we're not a couple, just good friends."

"So you don't fancy me?"

The bell pepper said, "Not really, no."

There was a tense pause.

Then the pinch of salt flung itself in the bell pepper's face. It was very lucky the pepper didn't have eyes, otherwise they would have stung quite a bit and the salt would have dissolved in the resulting tears. Nonetheless, the bell pepper screamed loudly.

And the manager of the hotel burst into the room.

"What's going on here then?"

He studied the situation and came to a sudden decision. Pointing at the open door he remarked coldly, "Assault and pepper, eh? Well, the holiday *seasoning* is over now, so get out!"

¶ Mustard try harder next time…

9 THE SHORT SENTENCE

A short sentence said, "Wait!"

"What for?" wondered a pendulum clock.

"For just a minute!"

"*Which* minute? I have lots!"

"Any you can spare," said the short sentence.

"Well, I suppose you can have this one, but it's second hand," offered the pendulum clock as it ticked.

"I thought the second hand was the minute hand?"

"The little hand is the minute hand," explained the clock. "The second hand is the third hand. Get it?"

"Not really, but thanks," said the short sentence.

The pendulum clock asked meekly, "Are you entirely certain you're a short sentence? It's just that sometimes I can't see your full stop. I know I'm a bit shortsighted and yet—"

"I must confess that I am mildly insulted by your remark, which tends to suggest that I have been deceiving you and the readers of this fable for reasons that probably are dubious and possibly felonious, and I wish most strongly to stress that I am now, always have been, and certainly intend to remain, to the utmost of my ability, for the entire duration of my lifespan, however long that may be, a very short sentence, and I will regard anyone who insinuates that the contrary is true with enormous rancour and I may even resort to legal proceedings to restore my tarnished reputation, so let this be a warning," said the short sentence.

"Oh, I'm sorry," sincerely apologised the pendulum clock.

¶ The minimum sentence for impersonating a short sentence is long!

10 THE UNFORGIVING TERRAIN

A shrew, a fox and a frog were crossing a limestone landscape of fissures and crevices. They were journeying from one forest to another, but going straight across the karst outcrop was the only feasible route. It was tricky ground for the animals to negotiate.

"I keep stubbing my toe!" groaned the shrew.

"And I get my paws stuck in the cracks," added the fox.

"The worst aspect of this region is the lack of surface moisture, which has all percolated underground," said the frog.

They pressed onwards and the sun beat down on them.

Tempers frayed and snapped…

"Bloody landscape!" cursed the shrew.

"Yes, it's an awful gross blighter!" agreed the fox.

"Moronic geology!" croaked the frog.

Suddenly a loud deep voice boomed from directly beneath them. "I'm not deaf, you know! I heard those insults and I'm extremely offended by them! In fact, I'm atremble with rage!"

The shrew, fox and frog were very contrite.

"Please don't punish us!"

"We wouldn't survive an earthquake uninjured!"

"We beg your pardon, sir!"

But the limestone landscape was unmoved by their pleas. Unmoved in emotional terms, I mean. In physical terms it shook itself so violently that the entire plateau broke into crumbs and the travellers were left bruised and battered among the sharp fragments.

¶ Limestone can forget but it never forgives.

11 THE SLOBBERY KISS

A walrus blew a slobbery kiss at a mermaid; she caught it and blew it at a passing ship; the ship kept it for a few hours and then blew it at a dolphin; the dolphin played with it until it got bored and then blew it at a jellyfish; the jellyfish thought it was a sarcastic gesture and didn't really want it, so it blew it at a squid; the squid was learning to juggle and tossed it up high in its tentacles but failed to catch it.

So the slobbery kiss was free at last! It drifted away.

Shortly before sunset it spied another slobbery kiss on the horizon that was coming its way, so it cried out:

"Isn't it a dreadful fate to be a slobbery kiss?"

"Why is that?" asked the stranger.

"Because we get blown here, there and everywhere!"

"Only if you are an old-fashioned slobbery kiss with sails to catch the breath of those who blow us. Look at me! I am a more modern slobbery kiss and I'm fitted with paddlewheels!"

"That's amazing! So you never get blown around?"

"Nope. You should upgrade too…"

"Are there *no* disadvantages?"

"Um… Now you mention it… My deck does seem to be infested with minstrels who play the banjo all night!

¶ Be kind to slobbery kisses, they have feelings too.

12 BRASSED OFF

"I'm really rather good at my job," said a wolf, but a wise sage overheard him and wagged a finger. "Never blow your own trumpet," he quoted. He then went back to meditating and levitating.

The wolf frowned and thought deeply about this advice. "He's right. I won't forget his words in a hurry!"

Talking about a hurry, the wolf was late for work.

He turned up at the concert hall with just a few minutes to spare. Then he took his position on the stage. The conductor, who was a pine marten, used his tail as a baton to keep time.

The music burst from the orchestra like an exploding simile!

It was Honey Empathy's *Sympathy in Bee.*

Are you familiar with that piece?

I'm not either. Anyway... Now was the exact moment when the brass section had to join in the music with their own instruments. But the wolf remembered what the sage had told him and he leaned quickly across to his nearest neighbour, who happened to be a rabbit. The rabbit saw what the wolf intended and tried to stop him.

"What are you doing? Get your paws off that!"

"Sorry," said the wolf, "but I've been told by a reliable source that to blow my own trumpet is wrong. So I intend to blow yours instead. If you like, you can play mine on my behalf."

"You buffoon!" wailed the rabbit. "I don't play the trumpet. I play the trombone. They sound utterly different!"

¶ Anyone seen my quote? It has a nibbled hood.

13 THE THIRTEENTH FABLE

"Why do I always have to be the thirteenth fable?" muttered the thirteenth fable in this particular sequence.

"What do you mean?" asked this sentence.

"It doesn't matter what collection I end up in," lamented the thirteenth fable, "even when they are written by flippant postmodern fellows, I still get the thirteenth place. I hate it!"

"But you *are* the thirteenth fable!" explained this paragraph. "I mean, if you were put in twelfth or fourteenth position you'd *still* be fable #13. I don't

154

see why you are getting so upset. It's your destiny, your essence, a fundamental part of what you are."

"No, that's not true. If was put in twelfth place I'd be the twelfth fable, and if I were put in fourteenth place I'd be the fourteenth fable. Take your cod philosophy and give it to the fish, but not to cod, throw it to haddocks instead, just for irony's bitter sake."

"My, my," said the next sentence. "Just be grateful you are the entire fable and not a mere sentence inside it, like I am. And *this* poor fellow is the thirteenth sentence in the thirteenth fable, so if there is any bad luck floating around he's going to come off worse and— argh! And there we go, he just fell over and died. So there!"

"Oh dear, you're right. I really ought to count my blessings," said the thirteenth fable in a chastised tone.

¶ One, two, two and a half... thirteen!

14 SENTIENT HOT-AIR JELLYFISH BALLOON!

A pterodactyl was flapping high over a volcanic landscape when it saw a jellyfish hovering in the air above a smoking volcano. "I didn't know that jellyfish could fly!" cried the pterodactyl.

"Nor did I until about an hour ago," came the reply.

"What happened? Please tell me."

"I was minding my own business in the ocean when a sentient hot-air balloon happened to float past high above me. I felt envy and wanted to be free like that. It occurred to me that if I could position myself over an active volcano, the rising heat would fill my canopy and I too could be a lighter-than-air aeronautical machine…"

"Great! But how did you position yourself over the volcano?" queried the pterodactyl as it glided in circles.

"I had to call in a favour and ask a waterspout to lift me up out of the sea and carry me over dry land to this spot. Then it dropped me into the crater and I filled with hot air and began flying before I landed in the pool of bubbling lava inside the volcano."

"What do you intend to do now?" asked the pterodactyl.

"I'm going to ask the sentient hot-air balloon for a date when it comes back this way," explained the jellyfish.

"Ugh! That's bestiality!" spat the pterodactyl in disgust.

¶ When you feel p-p-p-puckish, p-p-p-pick up a pterodactyl. Or don't, if you prefer. It's no skin off my beak.

15 BADDIE TWOSHOES

"I don't smink and I don't droke," said Baddie TwoShoes.

"You don't *what*?" questioned an owl.

"Smink or droke," repeated Baddie. He was a rare footwear komodo, made from two shoes joined sole to sole, with a blue tongue that flicked out to taste the air like that of a snake.

"I don't know those words, sorry," admitted the owl, but Baddie was daydreaming again and muttered:

"Just nitrogen really, with a tang of oxygen and a few inert gasses. I can't say it's bursting with flavour."

"What are you talking about?" asked the owl.

"Oh, sorry, I was just going off on a tangent. That happens often. My tongue constantly flicks out to taste the air and I supposed that the reader wanted to know what it tasted like…"

"Right, I see," said the owl.

"Carbon dioxide too and a little water vapour."

There was a lengthy pause.

"If you don't smink and you don't droke, what *do* you do?" wondered the owl. He was on his way to take part in a backgammon tournament and had stopped for a rest in a cedar tree.

"Good question," admitted Baddie TwoShoes.

"It was rather, wasn't it?" The owl felt pleased with himself, so much so that he forgot an answer was required. "Well, nice meeting you. Good luck with your future career. Bye!"

¶ Expect a point from swords and pens by all means, but you won't get one out of *this* fable.

16 TWO LETTUCES

Two lettuces were close friends. One of them went for a walk and got run over by a car while crossing the road. An ambulance came and took what was left of him to the nearest hospital.

Ten minutes later, the other lettuce received an urgent message telling him what had happened. He rushed to the hospital but the doctors on duty wouldn't let him into the room where his friend lay. "He's on life support and can't be disturbed," they explained.

"Life support? That's dreadful! How bad is he?"

"We are sorry to inform you that there's little hope of a full recovery. His body might survive but his mind—"

"He won't be a cabbage, will he?" gasped the lettuce.

"Er... no, but he *will* spend the rest of his life in a vegetative state. Not a cabbage, though. He's still a lettuce."

"Vegetative state? A *persistent* vegetative state?"

The doctors nodded. "It seems so."

The lettuce jumped for joy. "That's great news. He's fine!"

¶ Lettuce close our eyes and pray...

17 SEEING A GENIUS

A rabbit went into a public bathroom to freshen up. When he went to use the sink he was amazed to see a fox's face in the mirror. "How can this be possible?" he gasped. "He's not me!"

"Don't worry," replied the fox. "This isn't your reflection but a hole in the wall and I'm standing in an adjacent bathroom. I'm looking into your room because there's a genius in it."

"Where?" cried the rabbit. He looked over his shoulder but there was nobody behind him. The fox replied:

"You'll have to come round to this side and take a look for yourself. I think that's the best course of action."

So the rabbit left the bathroom and went into the one occupied by the fox and joined the fox at the hole in the wall. He peered through but there was only a weasel in the bathroom now.

"Is he the genius?" asked the rabbit.

"No, he's not. He only came in a moment ago."

"I can't see anyone else in there."

"Maybe I was mistaken," said the fox.

The rabbit went back to the other bathroom but as soon as he looked into the mirror above the sink, the fox roared, "He's back! The genius is back! I can see him very clearly…"

The rabbit looked over his shoulder but there was nobody there. So he hopped around to the fox's side of the wall and looked through the hole, but the only creature he saw was a vole.

"Is he the genius?" asked the rabbit.

"No, he's not. He only came in a moment ago."

"I can't see anyone else in there."

"Maybe I was mistaken," said the fox.

The rabbit went back to the other bathroom and yet again the fox was excited and cried, "The genius is back!"

"I'm not coming round to your side a third time," curtly answered the rabbit. He left the bathroom and went home and spent the evening using advanced mathematics to solve various mysterious of space and time. But when he went to bed, he thought it was a

159

shame that he never managed to get to meet the genius, if one had existed.

¶ The moral of this fable is that $(bunn)y=foxy^2$.

18 CUMQUATS

A prostitute named Marge was working her patch when a robot sauntered up to her. "What are you doing?"

"Working my patch," said Marge without pausing.

"I didn't know harlots were keen allotment gardeners," confessed the robot in surprise. "What are you growing?"

"Cumquats," replied Marge.

"Those are like little oranges, aren't they?"

"No, you're thinking of kumquats. Cumquats are quite different and I use them to give me intense pleasure."

"How do they work?" wondered the robot.

"I can't reveal details because that would be obscene, but they fill me with a special surge of ecstasy that only women in my chosen profession can ever hope to properly experience."

"Is there a name for that special surge?" asked the robot.

Marge nodded and answered:

"A whoregasm."

¶ That robot needed his crankshaft oiled.

19 SLEEPY UPRISING

The squirrel roared, "When are the people of Hiber going to wake up and become a nation?" His tone was passionate and his audience agreed that it was a dramatic speech. They applauded with their paws and hooves or whistled with their beaks. The squirrel acknowledged the reaction with a wave and dismounted the platform.

But an alligator approached him and said shyly, "I like the sentiments you expressed, but there's a flaw in your reasoning. You want the people of the province of Hiber to wake up?"

"Yes, yes, it's about time," replied the squirrel.

"Why is that?" asked the alligator.

"Because they've been oppressed for generations and only when they win independence for themselves will they be free to embrace the liberty that is the birthright of all beings."

The alligator cleared its throat and remarked, "If the people of Hiber wake up and become a nation, they will automatically be in Hiber Nation and therefore unable to wake up…"

The squirrel frowned. "I hadn't thought of that!"

¶ Hiber is a land of yawning chasms.

20 THE PLUMBER

There was a hippopotamus who was a plumber and very good at his job, but sometimes his old instincts got the better of him. One morning he was summoned to the house of a giant gastropod who was busy developing a clever way of winning at roulette.

"My toilet doesn't flush properly," said the gastropod as he answered the door. "Take a look at it for me. And while you're doing that, I will go back to my study and continue with my own work. Please don't interrupt me unless it's important. Thanks."

"No worries," said the hippopotamus.

The gastropod slithered to the study, so the hippopotamus went into the bathroom, where he soon discovered that the problem was with the cistern. He took the top off to examine it.

But the sight of a contained volume of water, even though it was very small, made him want to go swimming again. He couldn't resist the urge and so he climbed into the cistern.

But it wasn't strong enough to hold his weight and it broke off from the wall and crashed to the ground...

He tramped slowly out of the bathroom.

Then he gingerly knocked on the study door and when the gastropod called out, "Yes?" in a faintly irritated voice, the hippopotamus turned the handle and went inside and declared:

"I'm sorry to say that your cistern is floored."

The gastropod was mortified.

"My system is flawed? So there's no way I can guarantee that I'll win at roulette after all? How terrible!"

And he instantly tore up his diagrams and notes.

¶ Roulette is a wheely silly game.

162

21 CLOUD DISCO

A buttercup said to a fox, "Isn't it weird how the clouds seem to gather on the horizon at sunset? The sky above us is mostly clear but in the far west there are many clouds packed tight."

"The twilight sky is a disco, that's why," replied the fox.

"What do you mean?" asked the buttercup.

"It's obvious, isn't it?" said the fox. "Clouds often like to go dancing in the summer evenings. The dome of the sky is the dancefloor but only a few clouds are confident enough to go to the middle and strut their stuff. The others tend to linger on the edges."

"I wonder what music they dance to? Do you suppose it might be the music of the spheres?" cried the buttercup.

"That's classical music. I already told you that the sky at this time of day is a disco. It must be disco music."

"Name me some examples," pleaded the buttercup.

"I can't," admitted the fox sadly. "I can't think of any puns involving clouds and disco music, sorry. Maybe the reader can do that for you. I'm off to my own dance class now. Bye!"

"Really? Are you learning disco dancing too?"

"Nope, the foxtrot," said the fox.

¶ That's no joke, he really was.

22 THE TREE AND THE BEAVER

A beaver was always rushing around. "Hey, slow down," advised a tree that grew next to a stream. "Take a leaf out of my book and relax. I do almost nothing all day but look how tall I've become! You don't need to be a workaholic to succeed in life."

The beaver scratched his head. "Take a leaf out of your book? I don't see any books around here," he said.

"It was a figure of speech," answered the tree. "I did read rather a lot when I was your age. My favourite author was James Branch Cabell. But to return to the subject, I suggest—"

"So you don't have any books now?" the beaver interrupted.

"I got rid of them years ago."

"But you want me to take a leaf out of your book?" The beaver was so confused by this that he sat down to think. Then he had an inspiration. "I know what to do!" he suddenly cried.

And he jumped up and began gnawing the tree.

"What are you doing? Help!"

"It won't take long, I promise," mumbled the beaver through a mouth full of wood chippings. Eventually the tree fell with a mighty crash. With formidable energy, the beaver proceeded to chew the tree until it was all reduced to pulp. Then he spread the pulp out in thin sheets on the ground until the sun dried them and finally he stitched these stiff sheets between covers. The book was nearly finished.

But it still remained for him to gather all the leaves that had been on the tree and insert them between the pages of the book. Then he set down the completed volume, opened it at random, reached out and plucked the lucky leaf out. "There I've done it!"

¶ If anything, his life got more busy after this.

23 THE SEVEN Cs OF CCCCCCCRHYE

"I own the Seven Cs of Cccccccrhye," declared the business tycoon as he opened the double doors of a large warehouse full of machines, tools and assorted implements. "Take a look!"

"Can I swim in any of them?" asked the turtle.

"What do you mean?" sneered the business tycoon. The reason he was giving the turtle a tour of the facility was because he was vain and wished to impress as many beings as he could.

"The Seven Seas of Cry. I assume they are made from shed tears? But who shed them?" wondered the turtle.

"Numbskull!" growled the business tycoon.

"Have I misunderstood you?"

"Yes indeed! I didn't say I owned the 'Seven Seas of Cry', whatever *they* might be, but that I own the 'Seven Cs of Cccccccrhye', which are seven letters, all identical. In the word 'Cccccccrhye' the letter 'c' exists seven times in total. Do you see?"

"Do I sea?" frowned the turtle, perplexed.

The tycoon threw up his hands in defeat. "Whether you understand or not, I still own all seven of them!"

"If they are letters, shall I post them for you?"

The tycoon turned purple. "No!"

"But if you only own the Seven Cs of Cccccccrhye, who owns the rest of the word?" persisted the turtle.

The tycoon shook with rage. "Tonguewaggle Chipchop does!" he spat as he slammed the double doors shut.

Then he stormed off and left the turtle alone.

¶ I really have no idea why I wrote this fable.

24 THE CAVEMAN

Three friends were on a hiking expedition. When the sun went down they stopped to make camp for the night. To collect firewood more efficiently, they agreed to go in different directions and come back to this spot laden with fuel. So that's what they did.

They each had encounters while separated...

The first friend, who was an old fellow, met a monkey with too many cheeks. The second friend, who was an ancient tomb, met an earwig that was learning play the zither. The third friend, who happened to be an egg, met a caveman. When they all returned to the campsite, they shared their curious experiences with each other.

"Surely you felt at home meeting a caveman!" cried the old fellow and the tomb to the egg. "After all, you are the egg of a dinosaur and cavemen are also mainly prehistoric, aren't they?"

"This one wasn't," sighed the egg. "He was actually a man made from a cave. In fact he *was* a cave with gigantic legs and arms protruding from his sides and he strolled over the landscape like a weird troll. I didn't dare approach too closely. His mouth was full of stalactites and stalagmites for teeth and he looked pretty vicious…"

¶ And that's the ugly truth.

25 THE SULTANA

"I wonder what happens if you put current through a sultana?" mused the apricot. He had a scientific mind and was always experimenting with the laws of the universe; and once or twice he had nearly been arrested by a rhino cop for breaking a few of them.

"Good question. Shall we try?" replied the cashew that was his nutty assistant. Usually it's the professors who are nuts and their assistants who bring a dose of sanity into the laboratory.

"Certainly. Here's a sultana. I'll go and fetch the generator," declared the apricot as he rolled out of the room.

The cashew frowned. "What does he need a generator for? Here in my pocket is the perfect currant." His frown deepened. "Not that I have such a thing as a pocket, of course, but—"

He extracted the currant, laid it on the work surface and gently pushed it into the sultana. The currant moaned with pleasure and the sultana did too. So the cashew made careful notes.

The apricot returned with the generator, but as soon as he observed the scene on the work surface he dropped the valuable piece of equipment in astonishment. "What are you doing?"

The cashew ignored the crash of the machine and answered in a matter of fact tone, "My conclusion is that when currant is put through a sultana, the result seems to be truly grape sex!"

¶ There's no raisin to be shocked by what happened.

26 THE BATHTUB

"I've been around for a very long time," said the bathtub, "and some very famous people have immersed themselves in me. For instance, when the philosopher Seneca was forced to commit suicide by cutting his wrists, it was in me that he chose to do it."

"How impressive!" cooed the cold and hot taps.

"Yes, I've seen it all…"

The plug swung on its chain. "Was Seneca the most illustrious of all the people who ever bathed in you?"

"Successfully bathed, yes," said the bathtub.

"What do you mean by that?"

"Well, there was someone even more renowned than Seneca who tried to have a bath in me but failed."

"Why did he fail?" frowned the taps.

"Because he had the ability to walk on water, a miraculous power that enabled him to stroll across the surfaces of lakes and seas on his bare feet but proved to be a disadvantage every time he wanted to take a bath. No matter how forcefully he pushed down, his feet were unable to penetrate the surface tension of the bath water, so he could never climb into it. If he pushed down too hard, he would propel himself into a standing position, balanced right on top of all the suds."

"I bet that was the yeti, wasn't it?" cried the plug.

¶ As if yetis ever wash!

27 WHEN THE POT CALLED

"You're a liar!" cried the saucepan.

"How dare you?" gasped the frying pan.

"All that stuff about you learning to fly aircraft during the last war. It's utter rubbish!" sneered the saucepan.

"And who are you to talk? Were you ever really a mountaineer? I have a feeling that you probably weren't..."

"Gentle implements, please!" pleaded the pot.

But the saucepan and frying pan simply ignored him and continued to insult, belittle and humiliate each other.

"You never flew under the Golden Gate Bridge!"

"You never played chess with a yeti!"

"For crying out loud!" suddenly shrieked the pot. "Just who the hell do you think you are? Look at *my* achievements. I was an astronaut and spent a year of my life exploring Jupiter."

The saucepan and frying pan exchanged glances.

"What's a lump of hashish doing in the kitchen anyway?" they wanted to know. "He's a complete fantasist."

But the kettle chortled at this.

169

"That's like the pot calling the cannabis wacky!"

¶ The only real hero in that place was the soup spoon.

28 ME MARZIPAN, YOU JANUS

The god Janus, who had two faces, one looking forward and one looking backward, though neither could agree which was which, was eating some marzipan one day. The marzipan had come from the city of Toledo and it was delicious and I recommend you try it for yourself. Anyway, after all the marzipan had been devoured, one of Janus' faces turned to the other and remarked, "I have the face of—"

One moment… You're quite right, I apologise… The faces of Janus are fixed in place and therefore can't 'turn' to talk directly to each other. As a consequence of this unfortunate arrangement, they always seem to be muttering behind each other's necks.

But to return to the fable…

"I have the face of a famous actor," said the first face.

"Who exactly?" asked the second.

"Sean Connery," announced the first. "And you?"

"You mean, what kind of face do I have? Rather bizarrely, I have the face of Janus, the two-faced god."

The first face was amazed. "But Janus has two faces. If your face is the face of Janus it means—"

The second face replied, "Yes, my face resembles two faces. One of those faces looks like Sean Connery."

"And the other face?" demanded the first face.

"That one looks like Janus."

"So your extra face also has an extra face?"

"Yep, it would seem that way."

"Does that extra face also have an extra face?"

The second face said without emotion, "Of course. And so on and so on forever. This is called recursion."

"Oh my god!" exclaimed the first face.

"*Your* god? Me, you mean!"

"Yes, and me too!"

¶ It takes two, baby. Me and you. It just takes two.

29 MANY A SLIPPER

A cup of tea and a cooked fish were waiting at the breakfast table for the master of the house to sit down and eat them. Both were feeling sad at the thought of no longer existing in the world.

"I regret all the things I never did," sighed the cup.

"I regret the things I did do," said the fish.

There was a furious pounding as the master came down the uncarpeted stairs rapidly, impatient to be seated at the table and devouring breakfast. He ran only on his heels and missed a step.

He fell on his back, breaking it...

As convulsions went through his crippled body, his legs kicked out involuntarily and his slippers, which were too large for his feet, came off and flew through the air. Thanks to their trajectory, and we should always remember how much our trajectories do for us, they landed on the table exactly between the cup and the fish.

"Looks like you've both won a reprieve!" they said.

"Really?" gasped the cup.

"Yes indeed," answered the slippers amicably.

"But how? Why?" cried the fish.

"Well, don't you remember the saying?"

"What saying? Tell us!"

¶ There's many a slipper between a cuppa and a kipper.

30 A DONKEY'S HEAD

The bathtub said, "I know a story about Jesus that no one else knows. I happened to be around at the time."

"Tell us about it!" chorused the excited taps.

"Well," began the bathtub, "it's a very surprising fact that he rode into Jerusalem on the back of a lawyer."

"Why would he do that?" wondered the plug.

"Because the law is an ass!"

And the bathtub laughed so much at this own joke that he rocked from side to side and the water inside him sloshed over the rim and soaked the bathmat, who coughed pathetically.

Suddenly the window burst open and a donkey's large head thrust into the bathroom and cried, "Show a little more decorum please! People often get offended by wisecracks like that."

172

"Especially lawyers," commented the cistern.

"Why are *you* here?" frowned the donkey. "I thought a hippopotamus plumber broke you in an earlier fable."

¶ Why don't lawyers get arrested for soliciting?

31 PHOTO OPPORTUNITY

A rhino cop was walking the beat in the city where he lived and a tourist who had never seen such a thing stopped to take a photo of him. Because the rhino was in a reasonably good mood, he posed in a suitably dramatic style, with lowered head and gleaming horn. Then he snorted and made a noise that was loud and threatening.

The tourist grew nervous and stammered:

"Are you going to charge me?"

The rhino answered in a bellowing voice:

"Normally it would be a dollar per photo, but I'll make an exception in your case, because you're a badger."

"Thanks. My name is Bandit," said the tourist.

"A bandit! That's illegal!"

The badger shrugged. "Not where I come from."

"But I'll have to charge you…"

Bandit sighed and reached into his pocket. "How much?"

The rhino hissed, "Four jars of honey."

"I'm not *that* kind of badger!"

¶ Rhinos make good cops. They make them out of papier-mâché.

32 FORMS OF TRANSPORT

Three men who were named after forms of transport accidentally bumped into each other on a narrow stairway. One was going up, one was coming down, one was just loitering halfway.

"I have priority," insisted the first man.

"No, I do!" retorted the second.

"I was here first," pointed out the third.

The first man sighed and explained reasonably, "You don't understand anything. The reason I have priority is because I'm named after a form of transport. That proves it's logical that you must get out of my way and let me through. A form of transport, I say!"

"I'm also named after a form of transport," said the second man.

"Me too," added the third man.

"But this is incredible!" gasped the first man. "It's simply too much of a coincidence! I am John le Carré."

"Pleased to meet you. I am Joe le Taxi."

They shook hands. Then they looked at the third man, who cleared his throat with dignity and declared:

"Upstarts! I am Jeff le 'Orse'n'cart."

¶ Is there wisdom anywhere in this fable? Neigh!

174

A panther who lived in a rainforest prided himself on maintaining a dry sense of humour in moist circumstances.

His job was to raise funds to ensure that the rainforest was protected from interference by intruders. Half this money was spent on the repair and maintenance of a barrier that completely encircled the region; but in recent months other projects, such as the fitting of electronic alarms, had started to take a big percentage of the remaining half and it looked as if the cash set aside for the fence might need to be diverted before the end of the rainy season. It was worrying.

One morning the panther's boss, a panda, came to see him. "I'm very concerned about our budget," he said.

The panther nodded and replied, "So am I."

"The alarms and the guards and the surveillance cameras are going to cost more than expected. The temptation will be to use some of the funds set aside for the repair and maintenance of the fence on these other things instead. I don't want that to happen..."

The panther licked his lips. "Neither do I."

"So I want you to formally ring fence the funds allocated to the upkeep of the circular barrier," said the panda.

"You want me to ring fence the funds for the circular barrier?"

"I believe that's what I said."

The panther frowned. "But where will the funds to construct this new fence come from?" he asked. "I know! We can divert it from the money we intended to spend on those alarms, guards and surveillance cameras. Shall we make it out of bamboo?"

¶ Who knows if the panther was joking or not?

34 A BEAR CALLED TED

A bear called Ted was disparaging porridge when his Gran came into the kitchen and said, "I'm sorry to hear such foul language coming out of the mouth of a well-raised grizzly like you."

"I'm sorry," said Ted, "but I just don't like porridge."

"No bears *like* porridge. That's not the point. It's the food we must eat to keep the legends alive. Comprende?"

"I suppose so," muttered Ted.

"Why not go into the woods and find some berries? Then I'll bake you a delicious berry tart for dessert…"

"Into the woods on my own? Bloody hell!"

"You're quite ungrateful really," admonished his Gran. "I do so much for you but you don't appreciate it."

"Yeah, yeah." Ted stamped off into the woods.

It took him three hours to gather enough berries to make a worthwhile tart and when he returned to the cottage he was astonished to see how his Gran had changed. She no longer stood on her back legs. In fact she had no legs at all, just a long sinuous body and a sinister head with two fangs protruding from it. And she hissed.

Even more strangely, there was a bundle of something on the floor, probably old clothes, that looked just like an elderly bear that had been asphyxiated to death by a powerful noose.

"Here are the berries," said Ted, slamming them down on the table. "Hurry up and make the tart. I'm hungry!"

"Don't take me for Gran, Ted," said the python.

Ted threw up his paws in exasperation. "You're not still going on about that, are you? I *do* appreciate you!"

¶ Tarts made by snakes aren't tasty at all.

35 THE GAME SHOW

A pineapple said to a pear, "I have a great idea for a new game show and I told my producer about it and he has agreed to let me go ahead with the project! I've been given the green light."

"I didn't know you worked in television!" said the pear.

"For the purposes of this fable I do!"

"Well, what's your new game show going to be like?"

The pineapple could barely restrain his excitement. "Meals from many cultures and traditions will be asked questions on astronomy, maths, logic and other mind-blistering disciplines."

"Sounds fantastic! Does your show have a name?"

The pineapple nodded. "*Quizzene.*"

"Brilliant!" chortled the pear.

A mango appeared and approached them.

"This is my producer!" whispered the pineapple to the pear, but before he could formally introduce them, the mango came up close and said in a voice that was brisk and emotionless:

"Sorry, but I've had second thoughts about your game show idea and I've decided that I don't really like it."

"Oh no!" wailed the pineapple in acute disappointment.

"In cute disappointment?" queried the pear.

I leaned into the fable and said, "I didn't write 'cute', I wrote 'acute'. Why are you distracting the reader?"

"Sorry," said the pear, visibly prickled.

The mango ignored all this and added, "Yes, I think that *Quizzene* is actually a rubbish concept. So I want you to return the green light that I gave you. Hurry up, I'm in a rush!"

The pineapple passed the green light back to the mango, who took it and began to leave. But before he reached the end of this paragraph, he looked over his shoulder and said with all the slimy lechery of a typical middle-aged predatory fruit, "Nice pear!"

¶ They got married a few months later.

36 FOX IN SOCKS

There was a fox who rummaged through all his drawers for socks. He eventually found four of them and put them on. Then he went out and strolled into town to visit the art gallery.

But the people he passed on the street laughed loudly.

"Why are they laughing at me?" the fox wondered. "I'm just a fox in socks. There's nothing funny about that."

He entered the doorway of the art gallery and the ticket seller giggled and shook with mirth. "One ticket... tee hee! That will be 5 euros... heh heh! There you go, sir... ha ha ha..."

"What's going on?" the fox asked himself.

The gallery attendants and the few members of the public who were present also sniggered when they saw him.

"I just don't understand," sighed the fox as he stopped in front of the painting of a toucan. "What's funny?"

He was alone in this particular room, which was devoted to portraits of historical animals that were magicians.

Suddenly the toucan came alive and chortled:

"What a hoot! What a wheeze!"

"Why do you mean? What's so comical?" cried the fox.

The toucan gasped, "Socks... socks!"

"Yes, I'm a fox in socks. That's perfectly normal, isn't it?"

"*Odd* socks," the toucan spluttered.

¶ One was yellow, one was blue, one was purple, one was green. Two were up, one was down, one was halfway.

37 LEMON JELLY HOSPITAL

A raccoon was busy building a hospital out of lemon jelly. He made the bricks by pouring molten jelly into little moulds and after they had set he added them to all the other jelly bricks already in place. Very slowly the walls of the edifice rose higher and higher.

A passing triffid stopped and asked, "What's this?"

"Hospital in progress," said the raccoon.

"Really? You are constructing a facility for sick and injured creatures out of flavoured jelly?" gasped the triffid.

"That's exactly right," acknowledged the raccoon.

"The individual bricks are so small! And prone to melting! I bet you have been working on it for a long time?"

The raccoon nodded. "A very long time indeed!"

"It must take infinite patience?"

The raccoon looked horrified. "Oh dear no! That's far too many. There may only be a maximum of 350 beds in all the wards put together. It will have an outpatients department, though."

¶ Sure, that wasn't even a real homophone, or *raccoonophone* as the case may be. No need to point it out.

A rhino cop was called to the scene of a house fire. The house had been caught red handed, or red roofed, setting fire to a park bench. The rhino strolled up and said in a deep voice:

"What's all this then?"

"It's a case of arson!" cried the witness who had seen what the house was doing and had rung the police.

"That's not true," growled the house. "I was just stubbing out a cigar in this ashtray and it burst into flames."

"A park bench is not an ashtray, sir," said the rhino.

"Well, how was I to know that?"

"He's lying!" insisted the witness. "He set it on fire deliberately. It's a case of arson, I tell you. Arson!"

The rhino cop regarded the remains of the bench. "No one will be able to rest their arson that for a while…"

"So am I free to go?" asked the house.

"Wait one moment," said the rhino. "What's that I can see through the skylight of your attic? It's a suitcase."

"No, no, it's not! It's just a box!" wailed the house.

"Let's have a closer look, shall we?"

And the rhino went into the house, trudged up the stairs with difficulty all the way to the attic, found the suitcase and brought it back down. Then he opened it in the presence of the witness. Flames leaped out and danced like dancers who were made of fire…

"I told you so!" trumpeted the witness.

"Please don't play the trumpet in my ear," said the rhino.

"Sorry," apologised the witness, who happened to be a wolf. "A wise sage once told me never to blow my own and I must remember his words. But I *was* right. It's a case of arson!"

"You're coming to the station with me," said the rhino to the house. "It's illegal to lie about ashtrays in public."

¶ Rhinos make good ashtrays. They make them out of poachers' noses.

39 THE HEIGHT OF EVEREST

Everest was talking to a large spherical meteorite that had crashed into its summit and got stuck fast there. "Have I made you taller than you already were?" the meteorite asked, but the famous mountain laughed and replied as follows, "Not really, I'm sorry to say."

"But I'm at least four metres in diameter!" protested the cooling space stone. "And I'm perched here on your very apex, so surely I must add my own height to yours? If not, why not?"

"Because I'm not measured in metres, but feet," said Everest.

"So it's just a question of converting metric into imperial units? I can do that with my non-existent eyes shut."

"I'm sure you can," said Everest benevolently.

"One metre is 39.37 inches and there are 12 inches in a foot, so I am exactly 13.1233 feet high. If you were 29,035 feet before I landed on you, then your elevation must now be 29,048.1233 feet. I can't see any errors in my calculations," said the meteorite.

"I'm not measured in those kinds of feet," replied Everest.

"What kind *are* you measured in?"

"Yeti's feet. Including the length of the toes…"

¶ Mount Everest was only joking. The toes aren't included.

40 THE SANDCASTLE

An elaborate and enormous sandcastle saw a group of boys approaching with a football and it panicked. "No balls allowed on the beach!" it cried over and over again. "No balls!"

It didn't want to be accidentally smashed. It knew that ball games are very dangerous to sandcastles…

"No balls allowed?" questioned one of the boys.

"That's right. Don't you know the rules? On this beach, no balls are permitted. Tell all your friends!"

"We will," said the boys as they went away.

Later in the afternoon, a gang of girls appeared and started playing a game of cricket. "No balls allowed!" shrieked the sandcastle. But the girls ignored it and continued playing.

"Don't you know the rules?" wailed the sandcastle.

"Yes," answered the girls. "A group of boys told us earlier that balls aren't allowed on this beach at all."

"So why aren't you obeying?" spluttered the sandcastle.

At that moment, the ball struck one of the turrets and it collapsed onto a second turret, which also collapsed, starting a domino effect that made all the turrets and walls fall in ruins.

"Why did you disobey?" croaked the sandcastle.

"But we did obey!" came the answer. "No balls allowed here. We are girls, not boys. We don't have balls."

¶ What a load of bollocks.

41 THE VEGAN VEGANS

The star Vega can be found in the constellation known as Lyra. It is 25 light years distant from our sun, and on one of the many planets that orbit it exists a race of vegans. They are Vegans because they live on a world that revolves around Vega, and they are vegans because they avoid foods made from animals, including dairy products.

In fact they don't even eat plants, only minerals and radiation.

One morning at breakfast time, a female Vegan suggested to her lover that they have a cooked breakfast for a change.

"Sunbeams, for instance?" he said.

She shook her heads. "They are too light and leave me feeling peckish half an hour later. I want a substantial meal."

184

"Hmm, a cooked breakfast that is more filling than sunbeams... How about some lava from the nearest volcano?"

"I'm bored with lava. I want to try something new."

"So you are feeling experimental?"

"Yes I am! Why don't we try munching on that space stone I can see falling through our atmosphere right now?"

"Well, it has certainly cooked nicely with all that friction."

"I bet it's substantial fare too!"

"What do you imagine it might taste like?"

The female undulated her tentacles. "Not like a normal boulder, that's for sure. In terms of texture I bet it's—"

"What?" wondered the lover.

"Meteor," said the female.

¶ They put basalt pillars in comets, mount the comets in cones of dark matter and call them ice-creams. That's the kind of beings they are.

42 THE CINEMA SHOW

A recurring dream had a night off, so it went to the cinema and ended up watching a film that told the story of Freud and his relationship with his former disciple Jung. The actress Keira Knightley was in the film and it must be admitted that she's a beauty.

But the recurring dream didn't learn anything new from the story and he felt he had wasted his money.

So halfway through the film he went to see the manager to request a refund.

The manager was in the projectionist's booth and he happened to be an aardvark. The recurring dream said:

"You seem to have apricot jam on your—"

"Don't you dare mention it!" snapped the aardvark.

The recurring dream recoiled.

"Well, the reason I'm here is because I didn't like the film and I want you to return the cost of the ticket."

"Come now," said the aardvark. "It's a great movie!"

"You're joking, aren't you?"

"Not at all! Consider the themes and the way they are developed and the profound psychological insights provided by the script. The answers to many questions concerning behaviour, emotions, sentiment and other drives and instincts are provided…"

And the aardvark gestured through a little window in the booth that looked out over the crowded cinema.

"There! On the screen! Unpalatable truths revealed!" he cried.

But the recurring dream was unconvinced.

"You're projecting," it said.

¶ A good cigar is only a smoke but a recurring dream is a nightmare.

A hippopotamus who was a plumber was summoned by a Möbius Strip to fix a leak in a Klein Bottle that had got itself stuck in a sink. The hippo had recently swallowed a philosopher and was feeling unwell. "It was an accident and happened in the train station at Tenby," he groaned. "When I yawned, he jumped down my throat."

"I don't want to hear about that," rustled the Möbius Strip.

"Fair enough," said the hippo.

"Here's the Klein Bottle. Just repair him, will you?"

The hippo peered into the sink.

"Oh dear. That's a big job. Non-Euclidean geometry, you see. Always costs extra, that hyperspatial stuff."

"What are you talking about? It's just a Klein Bottle, a bottle with an inside but no outside. What's the problem?"

"It's the cost of getting hold of the right spare parts. I have to go into another dimension parallel to this one."

The Möbius Strip flexed his twist in exasperation. "Oh really! Can you tell me how much it's likely to cost?"

The hippo shook his head. "Not really, I'm afraid."

"But why the hell not?"

"Because the calculations involved are very tricky."

"Can't you give me an estimate?"

"I'd rather not. There are too many factors to consider."

"Not even a rough estimate?"

The hippo relented. "I suppose I can do that. One moment." He dipped into his bag and took out a pen and a sheet of sandpaper. Then he wrote the words 'X dollars' on the sheet. It wasn't easy to do this and the pen nib was worn away. "There you are."

¶ Hip, hippo, hurrah!

44 OUTREMER

A fox and a carrot that were really good friends decided to make a meal together. So they selected as many raw vegetables as they could find and chopped them up in a big bowl. Then they poured olive oil and balsamic vinegar on top and tossed the end result.

The healthy summery repast was ready…

But suddenly it jumped out of the bowl and went on the rampage and managed to conquer, thanks to its grasp of military strategy and tactics, a tract of land exactly equal to the Levant.

"No surprise in that really," remarked the fox.

"Why not?" asked the carrot.

"Because that was Salad Din-dins," said the fox.

The carrot sighed, even though he had no mouth, no lungs and hadn't paid his oxygen bill. "Dreadful pun!"

"What do you mean by that?" demanded the fox.

"Wordplay isn't your forte."

"The best forte in this context would be Krak des Chevaliers."

"No. *Wisecrack* des Chevaliers…"

¶ That punchline will be obscure to anyone uninterested in the history of Outremer. Too bad.

45 A GLASS OF WINE

"I really fancy a glass of wine," said a skeleton.

"You mean—" spluttered a ghost.

"Yes, I'm leaving you…"

"For a glass of wine?" cried the ghost.

The skeleton nodded. "Sorry. It's just the way I feel."

"So you don't desire me anymore?"

"It's just not working out," said the skeleton.

"I thought we were good together!"

"Not really. But I don't want to get into a debate. The situation is quite simple. There happens to be a glass of wine I'm interested in and I have decided to start a relationship with it."

The ghost's lips began trembling. "What's its name?"

"Dorothy," said the skeleton.

"And what does Dorothy do for a living?"

"She's a Cabernet Sauvignon 1953," answered the skeleton, "but in her free time she's a palaeontologist."

¶ How does one wine and dine a glass of wine?

46 RHYSOP'S FABLES

"What are you reading?" asked the newcomer.

The crow looked over his shoulder. "It's a collection of fables but they aren't traditional fables. They are postmodern jokes really. The entire set is called *Rhysop's Fables*," he said.

"Oh, a sequel to the present set of fables?"

"No, a prequel. There are 150 of them and they were written before the 57 that we are currently embedded in."

"Do we feature in any of them?"

"Yes we do," affirmed the crow.

"Are they amusing?" pressed the newcomer.

"Well, I'm not reading them for entertainment purposes. I'm seeing if there's any clue as to what might happen to me tomorrow. Prequels don't necessarily just deal with past events."

"Some are set in the future then?"

"It's difficult to be sure, but there's a chance they might be. I think it's wise to familiarise myself with them. That way I stand a better chance of avoiding potential disasters; and I might also get to learn something about my nature that I didn't know before."

"Will that also be true of me?" cried the newcomer.

"Yes, I don't see why not."

"In that case, will you take a look and find out?"

The crow agreed to do this.

He turned the pages and scanned them rapidly. Then he said, "It turns out that you're not a single individual but a list of many separate entities. How does learning this make you feel?"

"Intrigued," admitted the newcomer. "But what's on that list? Please tell me. I'm desperate to know!"

So the crow recited the list aloud: "A pig, a waffle, a box, a chump, a resentment, a caterpillar, a gift, a loom, a cuttlefish, an aurora borealis, a duvet, a chair, a sunken continent, a cup that runneth over, an ancient paradox, a snivel, a bone, a toothless cog, a piecrust, a passionate kiss, an aching thigh, a broken window…"

190

"All of them?" gasped the newcomer.

But the crow hadn't finished yet. "…a phantom, a cat, a bathtub, a chimney clogged with twigs, a forced laugh, a chewed pencil, a beetroot stain, a vague feeling, a hovercraft, an argument, a dog, an example of jargon, a butterfly, a solecism, a grotesque fiend, a coconut shy, a confident papaya and a thousand other things."

¶ A true renaissance newcomer!

47 WHEN IT LIGHTLY RAINED

A mongoose said, "I've just read the weather forecast in the newspaper and it seems we're due some light rain."

"What newspaper do you read?" asked the weasel.

"*The Daily Mustelid*," was the answer.

"You shouldn't believe anything you read in that rag!"

"It was just a weather forecast."

"They are no more objective about that than anything else. I tell you, the journalists on that paper are atrocious."

"Maybe you're right… Wait a moment, did you feel that?"

"No, I'm sorry to say I didn't."

"I felt a photon land on my nose. And another!"

"Ah yes," said the weasel. "So did I."

"Hundreds of them! Millions! A downpour of photons!"

"That's the light rain, I guess," sighed the weasel, "but I still wouldn't trust anything else you read in there."

"One moment while I fetch my watering can," said the mongoose. "I want to fill it to the brim with light."

"Stocking up for when there's an eclipse?"

The mongoose gestured at the newspaper. "That's right. They predict one of those for tomorrow at noon."

The weasel was exasperated. "You're so gullible!"

¶ The moon moved across my chest once. I didn't know why at first but I soon understood. It was a total eclipse of the heart.

48 REVERSING THE POLARITY

"Last night I reversed the polarity of a dreamcatcher," said a mandala to a crystal ball as they stood on shelves in a shop that sold magic, mystic and occult paraphernalia and adjuncts.

"A dreamcatcher? One of those constructions that look like a spider's web but made from twigs and string?"

"Yes," nodded the mandala, even though he didn't possess a neck. "I wanted to see what would happen…"

"And what *did* happen?" asked the crystal ball.

"Well, you know how a dreamcatcher catches bad dreams before they enter your sleeping head at night?"

"Sure, I've used them myself many times."

"What I discovered is that if you reverse the polarity, the dreamcatcher sucks the good dreams out of your mind and radiates them into the astral plane. I have no good dreams left."

"None at all? Can't you grow new ones?"

"I'm afraid not. Ah well!"

"How can you be so blasé about it?"

The mandala considered this question very carefully.

Eventually he said, "I suspect it's because I'm not actually alive. I'm a mandala. And you're not alive either."

The crystal ball sighed. "I should have seen that coming!"

"Didn't you?" frowned the mandala.

"Of course I did! I was just being modest. Things that aren't alive *are* allowed to be modest, aren't they?"

"Only if they are blasé about their modesty."

"Is this fable going anywhere?"

"*You* ought to know…"

¶ It's going as far as here. No further.

49 FLAMINGO SYNDROME

A man who was standing on one leg so that he could scratch his itchy left foot was apprehended by a vegetarian convex mirror, who said, "Why are you standing on just one leg like that?"

The man was something of a joker and replied, "I'm suffering from an obscure illness called

Flamingo Syndrome. This time tomorrow it's likely I'll turn pink and grow a pair of wings."

The convex mirror wasn't as surprised as it should have been. "That's a coincidence. I also have that illness!"

The man was taken aback by this casual statement. He lost his balance and because he didn't want to lose face as well, he fought the instinct to use his other leg to prevent the accident that was inevitable. He toppled to the ground and groaned as he lay there.

"Oh no, wait a moment!" said the convex mirror.

"What?" cried the injured man.

"My mistake," the convex mirror answered. "I don't have Flamingo Syndrome at all. I simply reflected *your* condition and I must have got mixed up and thought it was mine..."

"Does that happen often?" wondered the man.

"Yes. I'm a mirror, that's why!"

"Are you really a vegetarian?" asked the man.

"Indeed so. I can't bear reflecting scenes of butchery! One butcher I knew was so obsessed with his work that he cut off both his lower limbs with a cleaver and sold them as meat."

The man was amazed. "Double Flamingo Syndrome!"

¶ He didn't have a leg to stand on.

50 THE RADIOACTIVE LORD

"I am the Radioactive Lord!" announced the Radioactive Lord. He was aglow with self-satisfaction and radium.

194

"Don't expect me to shake your hand," said the beautiful girl.

"I expect nothing from you, my dear!"

The girl frowned. She was Ukrainian. "What do you mean?"

"It's what *I* can do for *you* that matters!"

"Hmmm. What's the catch?"

The Radioactive Lord grinned. "I am compelled by an old custom to be nice to you," he said. "It has been compulsory for radioactive lords to be generous to Ukrainians for many years, which is what I intend to start doing right now. Are you ready?"

"You're going to be generous to me for many years?"

"Um... no, you have misunderstood... It is the custom that has been around for many years. It has a name."

"What is that name?" demanded the beautiful girl.

"*Chernobylesse oblige*," was the reply.

¶ A convex mirror was once on amorous terms with a Ukrainian girl. Even though it was a vegetarian, it had a chick in Kiev.

51 THE RAVENOUS CROW

A crow flew low over a field and spied a scarecrow cycling slowly over the ploughed ground. The basket on the front of the bicycle was crammed with many different foodstuffs purchased from the market. The crow had experienced unexpected generosity from a scarecrow before, so he landed on the handlebars and said sweetly:

"Will you spare a piece of cheese for a bird?"

The scarecrow looked around. "Which bird do you mean?"

"Me, of course!" cawed the crow.

"Ah! But why should I give you any cheese?"

"I'm not fussy," replied the crow. "I'll be perfectly happy with olives, fruit or bread, if you'll donate them."

"That's not the point. Why should I give you *any* food?"

"Because I'm hungry," said the crow.

The scarecrow nearly fell off his bicycle. "You expect me to believe that you are the country called Hungary! That's stupid. Hungary is much bigger and flatter than you'll ever be."

"No, no, that's not right. I meant I was starving."

"You're a starling? Pull the other one. Where are your markings? You have all the characteristics of a corvid."

"Very well. Let me try again. I am ravenous."

"Ravenous? Partaking of the qualities of a raven? At last you appear to be speaking the truth! That's all it takes to get on the right side of me, you know. Here are a dozen satsumas…"

¶ If at first you don't suck seed, try spitting pips instead.

196

Three houses stood in a row in a street where many incredible things had happened over the years. On one occasion, the three houses were caught in a tornado and flung into a time warp. They travelled to the distant past but eventually another tornado brought them back. Two of them suffered some minor damage as a result of that.

And so now they were being repainted. One blue, the other white. The third house was still wearing his original coat of yellow. Once the task of painting was over, the builder told them sternly that they weren't allowed to move again until it had properly dried.

"No more tornado jaunts!" he warned them.

"So we're stuck here again," said the blue house. "How boring! I was looking forward to more time travel…"

"Me too," said the white house. "I mean, there are so many interesting periods of history for us to explore… The Ancient Greeks, the Sumerians, the early dynasties of China or Persia!"

"I doubt any of *those* will be as exciting as the trip we already had to prehistoric times," said the blue house.

"You might be right about that," said the white house.

"It was fantastic," said the blue house.

"Certainly was. And what we learned back there is totally at odds with orthodox wisdom about that remote era."

"Yes it is, isn't it?" agreed the blue house.

Then the conversation died…

The three houses waited. Time passed slowly.

The yellow house finally shouted in frustration: "Watching paint dry is like watching a dinosaur playing chess!"

"Shhh!" hissed the other houses. "Don't let the secret out!"

¶ A glass of wine happened to be in the area at the time and overheard. Luckily it wasn't a palaeontologist in its free time.

53 THE CAMPING EXPEDITION

"Let's go on a camping trip!" suggested the temporary shelter. He was a sheet of tarpaulin mounted on a pole.

"Great idea!" cried the driftwood fire.

"Shall I pack all our gear?" asked the portable stove.

"Make a list first," said the penknife.

"But we need to choose a destination before anything else!" pointed out the compass. The map nodded.

"How about the big city?" the temporary shelter asked.

The others were quick to agree to this.

"Brilliant! Let's go there!"

They drew up a list of the things they would need to make survival in the urban jungle more likely in case of an emergency: credit cards, shoe polish, neckties, mobile phones…

"I love roughing it from time to time!" squealed the map.

"Don't get into a flap!" said the penknife.

But they were all excited.

"Remember what to do if you encounter a salesman," the driftwood fire said soberly. "Don't make eye contact and don't run. Just speak to it in a low voice and back off slowly…"

¶ The rubber mallet was too busy to go with them. He had recently split up with his girlfriend and was hitting on tent pegs everywhere. He was clearly on the rebound.

54 CATEGORIES OF LOVE

"There are three main categories of Love," said the lips. The body was asleep and so the separate parts were free to talk about philosophy and anything else that interested them.

"I know amorous love quite well," said the heart.

"So do I!" chortled the pelvis.

"Amorous or erotic love… Eros," said the lips, "is one."

"What are the others then?"

"Philia is the second. That's brotherly love or love for friends. It's also known as Platonic love…"

"And the third category?" asked the eyes.

"Agape, or spiritual love," said the lips.

The ears spoke up. "I once knew two volcanoes who were in love. I don't mean that they liked to kiss and caress each other. It was more of a brotherly love. Philia, right?"

The lips nodded. "What happened to them?"

"Can lips nod?" queried the heart, but everyone hushed her. This often happened. They were heartless to her.

But to return to the volcanoes...

"The problem," answered the ears, "was that they lived on completely separate continents. One was in South America and the other was in Asia. They did send up smoke signals to each other by regularly erupting, but it wasn't always possible to see the plumes across such vast distances and so it was very frustrating for them."

The lips fell silent, deep in thought.

"Friendly love between continents..." they mused. "I wonder if that's a good example of Plato tectonics?"

¶ Yes, it is. I have no pout — I mean doubt — about that.

55 THEAKER PECULIAR

"What's a Theaker Peculiar?" asked the mouse.

"Ah, that's a rare subspecies of Theaker," replied the goat.

"How rare?" persisted the mouse.

"Very. Rarer even than a Blue Striped Skargill."

"But what's a Skargill?"

"A creature with many arms that lives in subterranean tunnels that it hacks out itself from the living rock."

"That sounds so cruel!" gasped the mouse.

"Yes, it would be much kinder if the Skargill killed the rock first, like gnomes do. But they don't."

"You are a fount of knowledge!"

"Not really, I use Google," chuckled the goat.

The mouse twitched his whiskers.

"I also have a confession to make," he admitted.

"You do?" The goat arched an eyebrow.

"Yes. I make them out of papier-mâché," said the mouse.

There was a pregnant pause.

"Look! There must be a male pause around here too!" said the goat as he pointed at the pregnant pause.

"A male pause? You mean a menopause?"

"If you like. But the females give birth to many little pauses at once. A litter of pauses! Enough to construct an entire lacuna, sometimes! They're an endangered species all the same."

The pregnant pause scurried away to safety.

The mouse blinked. "My confession is that I don't even know what an *ordinary* Theaker is," he sighed.

The goat laughed. "Ordinary Theaker? There's no such thing! There is only the Theaker Peculiar. It's an editor and reviewer. But it's so rare that you'll probably never meet one."

"A reviewer? Do you think there's any chance it will review the fables that we are currently standing in?"

The goat shook his head. "Nope. None at all."

¶ Theaker it here, Theaker it there, you won't find it!

"All aboard!" cried the captain.

And so the dead pirates trudged up the gangplank onto the ship. Not all of them were pirates, to be perfectly honest. Some of them were just ordinary rascals and ruffians, or unemployed highwaymen forced to do voluntary work by the government.

But they were all dead. Some were skeletons.

Others were xombies or ghosts.

That wasn't a misspelling. They weren't *zombies*.

Zombies aren't very bright.

Xombies are more intelligent and piratical.

'X' marks the spot, that's why. The spot of bother they might get into during a fight on the high seas.

Last up the gangplank was Gitsnack Chumpcracker.

He was the navigator, but he wasn't a very good one. He often tried to draw circles with the magnetic compass.

"Pull up the anchor, let down the sails, full wind ahead!" bellowed the captain. "I go to engage the enemy."

"I didn't know you wanted to marry the enemy!" gasped the first mate in consternation and disappointment.

"Yes, I'm sorry I didn't tell you earlier."

"So it's over between you and me? But... but... but why?"

"It's just not working out," said the captain.

"I thought we were good together!"

"Not really. But I don't want to get into a debate. The situation is quite simple. There happens to be an enemy I'm interested in and I've decided to start a serious relationship with it."

"Does this enemy have a name?" sobbed the first mate.

The captain nodded. "The Spanish Main."

"And what does this Spanish Main do for a living?"

"It is part of the coastline of Central America. But it spreads jam on an aardvark's nose in its spare time."

"The hussy! I'm not putting up with this. I am going to throw myself overboard. Goodbye forever! Glug!"

"But you can't drown. You're already dead!"

¶ The wedding went ahead. But the Spanish Main is secretly seeing the Barbary Coast.

57 SOUP OF FOOLS

The cauldron said, "I've invented a soup like no other. If you sip it, you'll instantly see everything from the point of view of any other being in the room with you at the time. Imagine!"

"I don't think that's a good idea," sniffed the spoon.

"Here, try some!" said the cauldron.

"Slurp. Yum! Ah, I was wrong. It's a brilliant idea!"

"What flavour is it?" asked the bowl.

"Aubergine with a hint of melted robot thumbs," said the spoon.

"That sounds dreadful!" said the bowl.

"No, it's delicious, I assure you!"

"Well, I disagree. I can't stand those flavours."

203

"Try some before you condemn…"

"Urgh! Argh! No, wait a moment! It's delicious!"

"I told you so, didn't I?"

"Yes, you did. You're amazing!"

"No, I'm not," The spoon was modest.

"But you are! I insist that you are!" cried the bowl.

"I'm not, I'm not!"

"Here, have some soup! Don't resist!"

"Glug! Hmm, maybe you're right. I *am* amazing."

"Told you so, didn't I?"

"Yes, I'm the most amazing sentient being in this fable!"

"Wait a moment! Don't get big headed!"

"It's just the plain truth."

"I was only being polite when I insisted you were amazing. You're an ordinary spoon really," said the bowl.

"Liar! Try some of this soup! There we go!"

"Eek! Oh yes, I agree with you."

"In fact," said the spoon, "I am so amazing that I am going to declare myself ruler of this room and all the beings within it. You must obey my every whim. My first command is to pour the remainder of the soup down the sink and then break the cauldron!"

"Hey thanks!" cried the sink.

But the pepper pot wailed, "Give me some first."

¶ When you see things from another sentient being's point of view, the end result is dictatorship!

THE END

Afterword

Because *Rhysop's Fables* was written in skewed imitation of Aesop, who not so long ago I read in an old Penguin Classics edition, the individual pieces gathered here do convey messages, but these messages are never upright and your life won't be improved by any of them. I'm thoroughly sick of being told how to behave by so-called 'wise men' and 'teachers' from the past, none of whom ever knew me personally. I refuse to inflict such glib pomposity on anyone else. Sort your own life out...

Not that I'm against messages embodied in fiction on principle. I just prefer ambiguity and choice to direction and control. When I read a story I find it more interesting if I can't work out the author's views on the questions of life. As a reader, I don't want to be passive, like a student attending a lecture; I want to grapple with the author, fight against him, jump any traps hidden in the prose and set my own in return. It should be an active pursuit, literature.

Anyway, I hope you enjoyed my fables.

If not, oops!